The ORIGIN
And Purpose of
Prayer

Rev. Dr. Caesar O. Benedo

THE ORIGIN AND PURPOSE OF PRAYER

Copyright © 2017 by Caesar Benedo

ISBN-13: 978-99919-2-443-4

All right reserved. No part of this publication may be reproduced, stored in a retrieval system, or transmitted in any form or by any means - electronic, mechanical, photocopying, recording, scanning or otherwise-except for brief quotations in critical reviews or articles, without the prior permission of the copyright holder.

Note: personal pronouns for God, Jesus and the Holy Spirit are lowercased in keeping with the different Bible versions used in this book.

Scripture quotations marked KJV are taken from the Authorized King James version © 1991 by World Bible Publishers, Inc.

Scripture quotations marked NIV are taken from the New International version © 1973, 1978, 1984 by the International Bible Society

Scripture quotations marked NKJV are taken from the New King James version © 1982 by Thomas Nelson, Inc.

Scripture quotations marked NASB are taken from the New America Standard Bible © 1960, 1962, 1963, 1968, 1971, 1972, 1973, 1975, 1977, 1995 by The Lockman Foundation

Scripture quotations marked NLT are taken from the Holy Bible, New Living Translation ®, copyright © 1996, 2004 by Tyndale Charitable Trust. Used by permission of Tyndale House Publishers. All rights reserved.

Scripture quotations marked ESV are taken from the Holy Bible, English Standard Version Copyright © 2001 by Crossway Bibles, a division of Good News Publishers

Scripture quotations marked AMP are taken from the Amplified Bible © 1954, 1958, 1962, 1964, 1965, 1987 by The Lockman Foundation

Scripture quotations marked THE MESSAGE are taken from THE MESSAGE: The Bible in Contemporary Language © 2002 by Eugene H. Peterson. All rights reserved.

Scripture quotations marked HCSB are taken from the Holman Christian Standard Bible © 1999, 2000, 2002, 2003 by Holman Bible Publishers, Nashville Tennessee.

Scripture quotations marked RSV are taken from the Revised Standard Version of the Bible copyright © 1946, 1952, and 1971 the Division of Christian Education of the National Council of the Churches of Christ in the United States of America. Used by permission. All rights reserved.

ACKNOWLEDGEMENT

A special thanks to the following people for their love, support and prayer to make this book a reality. Mr. and Mrs. Ononiwu, Mr. and Mrs. Ugwulor, Mrs. Sheyi Bonou, Pastor Fadel Akpiti, Mr. Samuel Fabrice Yomo, Pastor Samuel Kalu, Mr. and Mrs. Odjo, Mr. Kingsley Eme, Mr. and Mrs. Fajemirokun, Mrs. Vivian Asempapa, Mrs. Georgette Gbesset Baffoh, Pastor Veronica Bampoe-Darko, Pastor Maximo Deleon, Rev. Emenike Paul Ezechiluo, Rev. Lucile Sossou, Prophet Holy Joy, Rev. Dr. Nicaise Laleye, Rev. Alphonse Dagnonnoueton, Rev. and Pastor Mrs. Tigo, Rev. Isidore Godonou, Rev. and Mrs. Oluwaseyitan, Rev. Mrs. and Bishop Meshack Okonkwo and so on.

A million thanks to the members of my family for your love, encouragement, care, and support. May God richly bless you all.

I want to use this opportunity to express my appreciation to Pastor Benjamin Opeyemi Olaosebikan, and Pastor Eric Osei Yaw for their brotherly support, encouragement, and prayer.

A special thanks to Bishop Kwesi Adutwum for your love, encouragement, advice, support, and prayer. I'm indeed thankful to God for your life and for the incredible support you gave me. May God richly bless you.

A special thanks to Rev. Mrs Betty N. Coleman for your love, encouragement, support and prayer. May God richly bless and reward you for the great work you are doing for the kingdom.

I want to use this opportunity to express my gratitude to Pastor Zina Pierre for your love, support and prayer. May the Lord continue to bless you.

A special thanks to my Bishop, James Nana Ofori Attah for your love, encouragement, support and prayer. May the Lord continue to bless you.

I want to use this opportunity to express my gratitude to Apostle Michael Adeyemi Adefarasin for bringing out the best in me. I admire your commitment to excellence, your sincere desire to make a difference and your love for good work.

A special thanks to my papa, the archbishop Nicholas Duncan-Williams (founder of Action Chapel International), for your prayers, leadership, and spiritual guidance. May God continue to use you to raise and empower men and women to fulfil their divine purpose.

Words cannot convey how much I appreciate the love, care, support and prayer of senior deacon, and mama Georgina Lamptey for all the investment both of you made in my life. Thank you for standing by me at the very moment I needed it the most. May the Lord richly bless you.

DEDICATION

I dedicate this book to everyone who desires to know and understand how prayer came about, when and where it started, why it was established, the laws and principles that govern it, why humans pray regardless of who they pray to, and some effective techniques for consistent prayer.

Table of Contents

ACKNOWLEDGEMENT..III
DEDICATION...V
PRAYER 1
INTRODUCTION 3

Chapter One UNDERSTANDING THE CONCEPT OF PRAYER ... 7

Key Points 19
Laws and Principles of Prayer 26

Chapter Two   5WH PRAYER TECHNIQUE 29

What... 31
Important Questions 33
Who and Whom 37
Why.. 46
Where 57
When 66
How 72

Chapter Three   PERSONAL DEVOTION 81

Answers 82
How to Start Personal Quiet Time 86
Hints for Personal Bible Study... 90

Chapter Four MORNING GLORY PRAYER 93

Chapter Five   FAMILY ALTAR 97

How to Initiate Family Altar 100
Importance of Family Altar 102

Chapter Six   PRAYER RETREAT 105

How to Plan Prayer Retreat 112
Important Questions 113
Answer 113

Chapter Seven   PREVAILING POWER OF PRAYER 115

Chapter Eight   HOLY CRY 121

IMPORTANT ABBREVIATIONS 137

PRAYER OF SALVATION 139

PRAYER

Heavenly Father, in agreement with the Scripture that says the entrance of your word gives light and understanding to the simple (Ps.119:130), I beseech you to enlighten the eyes of my heart that I may understand the mystery of prayer as I read this book. Grant me insight and the grace to take hold of the truth, just as you did for Lydia in Acts 16:14, when you opened her heart to receive the truth spoken by the apostle Paul about your Son Jesus.

By the power of the Holy Spirit, I pull down every imagination, argument and thought that does not conform to biblical truths, concepts and principles that the wicked may want to use to hinder me from accepting the truth in this book. It is written that I shall know the truth, and the truth will set me free (Jn.8:32).

Dear Lord, open my eyes to the truth in this book and deliver me from the spirit of error in Jesus name. Amen!

Now Jesus was praying in a certain place, and when he finished, one of his disciples said to him, "Lord, teach us to pray, as John taught his disciples." 2 And he said to them, "When you pray, say: "Father, hallowed be your name. Your kingdom come. 3 Give us each day our daily bread, 4 and forgive us our sins, for we ourselves forgive everyone who is indebted to us. And lead us not into temptation."

(Lk. 11:1-4 ESV)

INTRODUCTION

When people say God is sovereign, he will act when he chooses to, he knows my needs, he is a loving father, he created me and he will give me whatever he planned to give me, he has the power to do whatever he chooses to do at any time, silver and gold belong to him and he gives them to whoever he wills, heaven and earth belong to him. I do not necessarily have to pray for him to act in my life, and so on, it implies they do not understand how God works.

It is true God is a loving father, and that he has the power to do whatever he chooses to do at any time. However, what many people don't understand about God is that he respects principles, and he would not violate his word for any reason.

When God speaks, it becomes a law says Dr. Myles Munroe. . From the very moment God said, "Let us make man in our image, in our likeness, and let them rule over the fish of the sea and the birds of the air, over the livestock, over all the earth, and over all the creatures that move along the ground," (Gen.1:26), he gave the earth realm to humanity and excluded himself in the daily management of earth affairs.

THE ORIGIN AND PURPOSE OF PRAYER

This simple act of God in the beginning legally put mankind in charge of the earth, and excluded God in the right to act within the earth realm without the cooperation of humans. Psalm 115:16 says the highest heavens belong to God, but the earth he has given to mankind. Once God gives a thing, he doesn't take it back declares the written word of God (Rom. 11:29).

Consequently, the only one who has the legal right (authority) to do things on earth is human (a spirit with body). John 4:24 informs us that God is spirit. And since God is spirit, he doesn't have the right to do things in the earth realm in accordance with scriptures and principles, without the cooperation of humans that he gave the earth to in the beginning.

Have you ever asked why the Lord Jesus, and John the Baptist taught their respective disciples how to pray? I believe one of the reasons is that there are laws and principles that govern prayer, which can only be learned through teaching. Whatever is taught can be learned. And the only way to learn these laws and principles is by teaching them. So that one can learn and use them to produce positive results in prayer.

If there is nothing to learn about prayer, the Lord Jesus, and John the Baptist wouldn't have taught it, and the disciples of Jesus would not have asked him to teach them how to pray. There is something you need to know about prayer, in order to be more effective. The knowledge you have about the subject determines the kind of results you produce. You can only talk about what you know.

INTRODUCTION

To be more effective and consistent in prayer, you have to know, and understand how God works, the principles that govern the heavens and earth, how the notion of prayer came about, and the principles on which it was established, why prayer cuts across all boundaries, how it was instituted and why humans pray regardless of whom they pray to. In addition, we need to know the basic principles and laws that govern prayer, and learn different techniques that make it work.

There is a saying that when the origin and purpose of a thing is not known, abuse is inevitable. We can't really make the most of prayer unless we understand its origin and purpose. Whatever exists has a purpose, and an origin. For us to produce better result through prayer, we need to understand the concept, why it was instituted, how it came about, how it works, the need to pray, and how to pray.

In my previous book, "Understanding the Art of Prayer (Revisited)," I addressed some of the reasons many pray without receiving answers, and what to do about it. We also spoke about what prayer is, why we pray, how to pray, the secret place of God, levels of prayer, rules of engagement, hindrances to prayer, mechanism of prayer, keys to effective prayer, dynamics of prayer etc.

There has been a lot of testimonies about how the book has impacted many lives since it was launched. At the same time, many have also asked me about the origin of prayer and why God instituted it.

THE ORIGIN AND PURPOSE OF PRAYER

Having explained what prayer is, why we pray, and how to pray, it becomes necessary for us to also understand how the concept of prayer came about, why it was instituted, how it works, and the principles that govern it.

The goal of this book is to add to what has already been done, cover new grounds, throw more light on other important prayer-related issues, and help others to enhance the effectiveness and consistency of their prayer life.

CHAPTER ONE

UNDERSTANDING
THE CONCEPT OF PRAYER

In my previous book on prayer, I mentioned that prayer is one of the most taught subjects in the Christendom because of its importance. However, it is perhaps the most misunderstood. More work has been done on the *need to pray* than on *how to pray*. Most of us know we need prayer and we can give many reasons why we have to pray. The major problem Christians are facing today is the proper understanding of the *how-to* of prayer. To produce better results through prayer, you have to know the techniques that work.

Apart from understanding the *how-to* of prayer, it is very important that we understand how pray came about, the principles on which it is established, and the laws that govern it. To do this, we must return to the book of Genesis where everything started.

Genesis1:1-25, recounts how God created all the beautiful things we see in the world today. The passage also points out that God saw the things he had created and that they were good.

THE ORIGIN AND PURPOSE OF PRAYER

In verse 26, God said, "Let us make man in our image, after our likeness. And let them have dominion over the fish of the sea and over the birds of the heavens and over the livestock and over all the earth and over every creeping thing that creeps on the earth."

We notice in the passage that when God created everything, he took part in the work, but when it comes to the management of earth affairs, he handed it over to humans and removed himself in the dominion mandate. He said, "Let them have dominion…" By this, God made the earth human's domain, territory or jurisdiction and made human race the governor and manager of the earth.

The heavens belong to the Lord, but he has given the earth to all humanity.
(Ps.115:16NLT)

I think one of the reasons God gave the earth to humans is that it was not intended for spirit being, since no spirit can dwell legally on earth without a body. In fact, nature demands that every living being, including animals coming to this planet must go through the womb (born), in order to gain legitimacy on earth. Otherwise, it will be cursed for breaking the rules of nature.

Genesis1:2 shows how the Spirit of God hovers over the surface of the waters. He couldn't dwell on earth because there was no human body for him to dwell in. For God to make man legal on earth, he had to form a body for him.

Then the Lord God formed the man of dust from the ground and breathed into his nostrils the breath of life, and the man became a living creature. And the Lord God planted a garden in Eden, in the east, and there he put the man whom he had formed.
(Gen.2:7-8ESV)

UNDERSTANDING THE CONCEPT OF PRAYER

The earth was formless and empty, and darkness covered the deep waters. And the Spirit of God was hovering over the surface of the waters.
(Gen.1:2NLT)

And afterward, I will pour out my Spirit on all people. Your sons and daughters will prophesy, your old men will dream dreams, your young men will see visions. Even on my servants, both men and women, I will pour out my Spirit in those days.
(Joel 2:28-29NIV)

Looking at the three passages above, I would like to ask a few questions. First, why did God had to form a body for the man he created in Genesis1:26-27? Second, why could the Holy Spirit not dwell on earth in the beginning? Third, did God give the earth to humanity in Genesis1:2 or 1:26-28? Fourth, why did God promise to pour him (Holy Spirit) on humans? Fifth, why can't the Holy Spirit dwell on earth without a body? Sixth, why did God make our body the dwelling of his Spirit? Please mediate on these questions.

Although, God made the earth human's domain, puts mankind in charge of earth affairs, gave us the right to act on earth, and excluded himself from the mandate, he remains the visionary. Genesis2:15 says he took the man and put him in the Garden of Eden to work it and take care for it. For God to achieve his plan on earth, he has to work through humans who he gave the right to do things on earth.

He determines the number of the stars and calls them each by name.
(Ps.147:4NIV)

THE ORIGIN AND PURPOSE OF PRAYER

Lift your eyes and look to the heavens: Who created all these? He who brings out the starry host one by one, and calls them each by name. Because of his great power and mighty strength, not one of them is missing.
(Is.40:26NIV)

The two scriptures above highlight the divine principle of naming things as a means of identification. The first says God counts the stars and calls every one of them by name, while the later declares that he created the stars, brings them out one after another, calling each of them by name, because of his great power. This suggests that when the Lord created the things in heaven, he gave them names as way of identification.

Nonetheless, when he formed all the wild animals and the birds of the earth from the ground, the Bible says he brought them to the man he gave the right to do things on earth to see what he would call them, and whatever name Adam gave to the living creatures remain their names till today.

So out of the ground the Lord God formed every beast of the field and every bird of the heavens and brought them to the man to see what he would call them. And whatever the man called every living creature, that was its name. The man gave names to all livestock and to the birds of the heavens and to every beast of the field. But for Adam there was not found a helper fit for him.
(Gen.2:19-20ESV)

Why would God bring the animals he formed from the earth to the man to name them? Why couldn't he name them by himself as he did to the stars he created in heavens?

UNDERSTANDING THE CONCEPT OF PRAYER

Why would he seek permission from the man? The simple answer to these questions is that God gave the right to act on earth to humans, and he won't do anything in the earth realm without the cooperation or permission of human being.

Otherwise, he would violate his word and the principles he established in the beginning. He made the heavens his dwelling and the earth human's territory. God has both the ability to do things (power), and the right to act (authority) in heaven, he gave the right to act (authority) on earth to humans when he made us governors of the earth and he won't violate the order.

In other words, God has the power to do things, but the right to exercise it on earth belongs to humankind. This means God won't do anything in the world without humans giving him the authorization. And since he remains the visionary, he devised a means that he could use to obtain the right to act legally in the world from mankind. So that, through this medium, he can interfere and work on earth legally.

This medium is what we call "Prayer." That is to say, prayer is the only means by which humans give spirit beings, whether the living God or demons, the right to act in the earth realm; through the authority God conferred on humankind in the beginning when he made us the governor of the earth.

Prayer becomes the spiritual bridge that connects the spirit world and the earth. It is the only means by which God's ability to do things connects with the right of humans to act on earth to effect changes amongst mankind. Prayer is the only weapon that connects the heaven, and the earth.

THE ORIGIN AND PURPOSE OF PRAYER

God has the ability (power) to do things, but humankind retains the right (authority) to act on earth. Prayer connects God's power with the authority of human to change things in the world.

It came about as a result of the structure and order that God established in the beginning between the heavens, and the earth. The heavens is God's habitation, while the earth is man's territory. The order is that no spirit can act on earth without the cooperation or permission of humans who God put in charge of the earth realm.

The Lord retains both the ability to do things and the right to act in heaven. He doesn't need anyone's approval or permission to work in heaven. But on earth, he needs the invitation or authorization of humans to do things. This is why heaven needs our prayers. Heaven does not respond to the earth until prayer goes up, says my papa the archbishop Nicholas Duncan-Williams.

Anytime there is a call for prayer, know that God is seeking the right to do things amongst humans, and he can only obtain it through the prayer of the church. No spirit being can interfere with earth affairs or act in the earth realm without the prayers of humans that give them the right to do things in the world. This is why prayer cuts across all boundaries, be it religion, language, culture, race, geographical location, social ranks, and so on.

I like the way Dr. Myles puts it, "The president of the United States does it, the Prime Minister of Israel does it, the Chairman of the Palestinian People does it, and the Queen of England does it. Jews do it, Muslims do it, Hindus do it, Buddhists do it, pagans do it, heathens do it, Christians do it, everyone does it.

UNDERSTANDING THE CONCEPT OF PRAYER

Few are sure it works, and even less believe it is necessary What is it? Prayer!"

Everybody prays, regardless of whom they pray to. Few are sure prayer works, while some don't believe it is necessary. In the end, almost everyone prays to something. And the spirit a nation, people or region prays to controls that territory, because through prayer, the legal right to act on earth that God gave to humans is given to spirit beings.

The devil led him up to a high place and showed him in an instant all the kingdoms of the world. And he said to him, "I will give you all their authority and splendor, for it has been given to me, and I can give it to anyone I want to. So if you worship me, it will all be yours." (Lk. 4:5-7NIV)

Satan said in the above passage that both the right to act in the earth realm (authority), and the splendor has been given to him, and he could give it to whoever he wills. The fact is that when God gave the dominion mandate to humans, Satan deceitfully stole the right of rulership from Adam in the beginning through deception and manipulation, and as long as the seeds of Adam live on earth, Satan holds it on lease.

For Satan to say to Jesus that he would give him the authority (right to act), and the splendor of the earth, is because mankind ceded it to him. However, through the sacrificial work of Jesus Christ on the cross, he disarmed Satan and took from him, the authority he stole from humans and gave it to the church, which is his body to exercise on earth. For more information on this, please go to my book, *Understanding the Art of Prayer (Revisited)*, under the heading "Rules of Engagement."

THE ORIGIN AND PURPOSE OF PRAYER

I like using some analogies when teaching about the concept of prayer. One of the examples I think people easily identify with is that of a parent who knocks at the door of their teenager, and wait till the child opens the door before entering their room. You will notice that even though the parents own the house and everything in it, from the very moment they gave their son or daughter the little room, they have to knock anytime they want to enter their child's room, especially when the child attains a certain age.

Whenever you knock at your son or daughter's door, you are seeking their authorization or permission to enter their space. If you fail or forget to knock before entering, your child may look at you and say something like, "Dad, or Mom, you didn't knock!" What they are indirectly saying is that you didn't seek their authorization before entering their room. The reason is that, though you own the house, the little room you gave them, becomes their space, domain, territory or jurisdiction.

No matter what happens in the room, if your child doesn't call your attention to it, you won't act or intervene. And anytime your child calls your attention for something in the room, he gives you the right to act within his space or jurisdiction. There could be an instance when you notice something that need to be fixed in the room, what majority do is to discuss it with their child before taking any action. We do all these for them to give us the right to act in their territory, through the authority we gave them when we made the room their domain. In other words, you knock to get the permission to enter their space.

UNDERSTANDING THE CONCEPT OF PRAYER

The same principle applies to the earth. In that, God created everything, he gave the earth to humans and excluded himself in the dominion mandate. From the moment the Lord gave the authority over the earth to humans, he won't intervene in earth affairs without the cooperation of humans. No matter what happens on earth, the Lord will not step-in unless somebody calls his attention through prayer. If he ever steps-in without the permission of humankind, he would violate his principles and the order he established between the heavens and earth. We pray to call his attention to earth affairs and give him the right to act on earth through the authority he gave to humans in the beginning.

Another good example is a rented apartment. When you sign a contract and pay all that the house owner demands, the apartment becomes your domain. Once you start living in it, the house owner loses the right to do things in the apartment without your permission. No matter what happens in the apartment, the house owner cannot do anything without your invitation. Just as it is with the house owner and the rented apartment, that is how it is with God and the earth. The Lord created the earth and gave it to humans. He won't act in the world without the cooperation of humankind.

The last example I would like to use is that of a boss and their employees. Why would the person who builds his company, employs you, gives you an office and pays your salary, knock at your door anytime he or she is coming into your office? It is simply because your office is your space and only you retain the right to act in it

THE ORIGIN AND PURPOSE OF PRAYER

As long as it remains your personal office, anyone coming in have to seek your permission to do things within your space. Your boss has the power but you retain the right to act within your jurisdiction regardless of the size of your office.

Just as your boss, house owner or parents needs your permission or cooperation to act within your space, God does the same to act on earth. I gave these three examples to explain the notion of prayer. Prayer is a necessity! It came about as a result of the structure and order that God established between the heavens and earth. It bridges the two worlds. God is the visionary who has a perfect plan for the earth that he gave to humans to manage. It takes prayer for him to interfere in earth affairs. Prayer allows the spirit world to impact the earth.

Heaven does not respond to the earth until prayer goes up. God cannot do anything for humanity until somebody prays, for it is illegal for him to come to the earth to do anything without invitation through prayer because he gave the earth to mankind.

- Archbishop Nicholas Duncan-Williams

Anytime your boss, house owner or parent tries to enter your space without your authorization, they violate your privacy and space. Whenever they enter without knocking and you say something like "But you didn't knock," you are indirectly questioning their right to enter your space without your authorization.

Likewise, whenever God calls for prayer, he is seeking our permission to act on earth.

UNDERSTANDING THE CONCEPT OF PRAYER

Prayer is the only means or medium through which God's ability to do things connects with the right of man to act in the world to produce the miraculous and effect changes in the world. Prayer is you giving God the right to manifest his power in your life. It is necessary for divine intervention on earth.

Let me say here that God knows what you are going through, he knows that things are not going on well with you, he knows the enemies are trying to mess-up your marriage, relationship, career, children, health, finance, business, destiny, project, education etc., but there is nothing he can do unless you pray.

You may say, but God is sovereign! And sovereignty implies independent or freedom from external influence. Why would he wait till I pray before he moves on my behalf when he can do whatever he chooses to do at any time? It is true that God is sovereign. However, the Lord is as sovereign as his word. Psalm138:2b says, "You have magnified your word above all your name." This means that when God speaks, he submit himself to his word.

While speaking on the *Purpose for Prayer,* Dr. Myles says, "God is as sovereign as his word, he is limited by his word, and he will never violate his word." He adds, "Whenever God speaks, whatever God says becomes law. Not only to creation but it becomes law also to God. God is sovereign until he speaks."

From the moment God said in Genesis1:26, "Let them have dominion…" the word became law, and it established the boundary that limits God's activities in the earth realm.

THE ORIGIN AND PURPOSE OF PRAYER

By reason of this word, the right to act on earth belongs to humans (spirit with body). All spirit beings must be authorized by humans to act legally on earth. The only way we authorize spirit beings to act in the earth realm is through prayer.

Prayer was created by the limitation of God's word, say Dr. Myles. Had God not given the dominion mandate to humans, there wouldn't have been any limit to his activities on earth. It is the boundary that his word established in the beginning as it relates to earth affairs, which denies spirit beings the right to act legally in the earth realm that gave room to prayer. So that through prayers, humans can either grant or deny spirit beings the right to work on earth.

And when you pray, do not be like the hypocrites, for they love to pray standing in the synagogues and on the street corners to be seen by men. I tell you the truth, they have received their reward in full. But when you pray, go into your room, close the door and pray to your Father, who is unseen. Then your Father, who sees what is done in secret, will reward you. And when you pray, do not keep on babbling like pagans, for they think they will be heard because of their many words. Do not be like them, for your Father knows what you need before you ask him. "This, then, is how you should pray: ..."
(Matt. 6:5-9NIV)

The above passage shows God knows what we need before we ask him. He knows everything that concerns us, both the good and the bad. He sees our struggles, challenges, difficulties, trials, pains, frustration, tears, weakness, lack, desires, etc. and he has the power to change our situations if only we can give him the right to act in our lives. The easiest way to do it is to pray.

UNDERSTANDING THE CONCEPT OF PRAYER

Are you going through negative situations, does it look like your world is coming to an end, does it seems like hell has broken loose and you don't know what to do? Cry out to the Lord today in prayer. Connect his ability to change lives and situations with your right to act in life, and change the course of your destiny. It is possible! It is not too late! You can make it happen today, through prayer. Arise and pray!

KEY POINTS

1. God is spirit
2. He is as sovereign as his word
3. When he speaks, it becomes law
4. The heavens is his dwelling
5. He created the heavens and earth (visionary)
6. He made the earth to be inhabited by humans (spirit with a body)
7. He gave humankind the right to govern it
8. He excluded himself in the management of earth affairs
9. There are principles that govern heavens and earth affairs
10. He respects the principles and protocol he puts in place regarding earth affairs
11. He cannot intervene in earth affairs without the cooperation of humans
12. He has both the ability to do things, and the right to act in heaven
13. He granted the legal right to do things on earth only to humanity

THE ORIGIN AND PURPOSE OF PRAYER

14. Prayer bridges and connects the two worlds (heaven and earth)

15. Prayer authorizes God to act and work on earth

16. Prayer is the only instrument a human can use to provoke divine intervention

17. Prayer is the only means through which humankind either grant or deny spirit beings, whether the living God or demons, the right to act in the earth realm

18. Prayer came about as a result of the order and structure that God established between the heavens and earth

19. We pray to give God the right to do things on earth through the authority he gave to humanity in the beginning when he puts us in charge of earth affairs

20. Prayer is the meeting place between humanity, and divinity

21. Prayer is the womb that births God's agenda and causes his reign to manifest on earth

22. Prayer gives humans access to the spirit world, and grant spirits the right to enter and work in the earth realm

God uses the prayer of the church to birth his agenda and establish his will on earth. He does nothing on earth without the prayer of Saints. Churches move his hand through prayer to work among humans.

God won't bypass the authority he gave mankind over the earth, neither will he interfere with human affairs unless someone invites him. We pray to give heaven access and permission to act in this world that lies in wickedness. Prayer came to being because of the structure and order God puts in place between heaven and earth.

UNDERSTANDING THE CONCEPT OF PRAYER

The order is, the heavens belong to God, while the earth has be given to humanity. The Lord freely gave the right to act (authority) on earth to humans in the beginning when he said, "Let they have dominion …" This made humans the only being that has the right to exercise authority on earth.

Nature demands that every living being coming to this world, whether humans or animals pass through the womb or be born to gain legitimacy on earth. No spirit can fully live and act on earth without a human body. When a person dies, his spirit leaves the earth or becomes an illegal occupant. It is the body that keeps the spirit legal on earth.

Whenever I teach on this subject, I often ask those in my class how they would define prayer to a four years old child. In response, some would say, "Prayer is an act of communication or talking with God." If prayer is an act of communication with God, it means that the notion of prayer came to being in the Garden of Eden.

When the Lord brought the animals and birds he formed to Adam in the garden to see what he would call them, the Bible only says whatever Adam called each living creature remains its name till today. It is quite possible Adam spoke with God, but the Scripture didn't record his words (Gen.2:19-20).

Following the simple definition of prayer by those in my class, which says communication or dialogue only takes place when there is exchange of information between two or more persons, we can establish that the notion of prayer was born in the Garden of Eden,

THE ORIGIN AND PURPOSE OF PRAYER

after the fall of mankind. Since the Bible records the full account of the first dialogue or communication between God and humanity in Genesis chapter three.

Now the serpent was more crafty than any of the wild animals the Lord God had made. He said to the woman, "Did God really say, 'You must not eat from any tree in the garden'?" The woman said to the serpent, "We may eat fruit from the trees in the garden, but God did say, 'You must not eat fruit from the tree that is in the middle of the garden, and you must not touch it, or you will die.'" "You will not surely die," the serpent said to the woman. "For God knows that when you eat of it your eyes will be opened, and you will be like God, knowing good and evil." When the woman saw that the fruit of the tree was good for food and pleasing to the eye, and also desirable for gaining wisdom, she took some and ate it. She also gave some to her husband, who was with her, and he ate it. Then the eyes of both of them were opened, and they realized they were naked; so they sewed fig leaves together and made coverings for themselves. Then the man and his wife heard the sound of the Lord God as he was walking in the garden in the cool of the day, and they hid from the Lord God among the trees of the garden. But the Lord God called to the man, "Where are you?" He answered, "I heard you in the garden, and I was afraid because I was naked; so I hid." And he said, "Who told you that you were naked? Have you eaten from the tree that I commanded you not to eat from?" The man said, "The woman you put here with me — she gave me some fruit from the tree, and I ate it." Then the Lord God said to the woman, "What is this you have done?" The woman said, "The serpent deceived me, and I ate."
(Gen 3:1-13 NIV)

UNDERSTANDING THE CONCEPT OF PRAYER

When God came to visit Adam in the garden, in the cool of the day, his sweet presence that humankind normally enjoyed anytime the Lord comes to fellowship with Adam became a treat and danger to humanity because sin robbed him of his glory and position. Adam and his wife ran and hid from the Lord God among the trees of the garden because they were afraid of God.

The Lord asked Adam where he was because he couldn't find him at the very place he normally meets him. My reason is that God didn't looked for Adam in chapter 2 when he brought the animals for him to name. "Where are you?" the Lord asked him. "I heard your voice in the garden, and I was afraid because I was naked; and I hid myself" said Adam. "Who told you that you were naked? Have you eaten from the tree of which I commanded you that you should not eat?" the Lord asked him.

I love the way one of my friends used what happened at the mount of transfiguration to illustrate Adam's situation. He said the Lord Jesus had to move from the natural to a higher dimension before Moses and Elijah who were already in glory could appear to him and spoke about the mission he was about to accomplish at Jerusalem.

Now about eight days after these sayings he took with him Peter and John and James, and went up on the mountain to pray. And as he was praying, the appearance of his countenance was altered, and his raiment became dazzling white. And behold, two men talked with him, Moses and Eli'jah, who appeared in glory and spoke of his departure, which he was to accomplish at Jerusalem. Now Peter and those who were with him were heavy with sleep, and when they wakened they saw his glory and the two men who stood with him.

THE ORIGIN AND PURPOSE OF PRAYER

And as the men were parting from him, Peter said to Jesus, "Master, it is well that we are here; let us make three booths, one for you and one for Moses and one for Eli'jah" - not knowing what he said. As he said this, a cloud came and overshadowed them; and they were afraid as they entered the cloud. And a voice came out of the cloud, saying, "This is my Son, my Chosen; listen to him!"
(Lk.9:28-36RSV)

The passage says while Jesus was praying, his face changed and his clothes became dazzling white. Suddenly Moses and Elijah appeared to him in glory and started talking with him. Although, the Lord had Peter, James and John with him, none of they could speak with Moses and Elijah because they were in another dimension. Had Jesus not prayed his way into that higher dimension, perhaps he wouldn't have encountered the two great men in glory. He had to be in glory to attract those who were already in it.

Sin brought Adam down from glory, robbed him of his position, created a huge gap between him and God, drove him far away from God's presence and caused him to hide among the trees of the forest.

In an attempt to reestablish the connection, amplified man's voice, restore him to his position, and maintain the relationship, the Lord God introduced the use of sacrifice in the process. Verse 21 says God made tunics of skin, and clothed them. Many believe that God killed an animal (lamb), and used the skin to make garments for Adam and his wife because they were both naked.

UNDERSTANDING THE CONCEPT OF PRAYER

All we are saying is that the concept of prayer was born in the Garden of Eden, after the fall of mankind. Due to the gap and separation that sin established between God and human race, the Lord introduced the use of sacrifice to bring mankind back to our position, reestablish the broken connection that sin destroyed, since Adam and his wife were both fleeing God's presence.

When God drove man out of the garden, the use of animal and fruit sacrifices became part of the prayer process as we observe in the case of Cain and Abel. Cain brought an offering of the fruits of the soil to the Lord, while Abel brought of the firstborn of his flock. After the offering, God spoke to Cain as we see in the passage below.

Now Adam knew Eve his wife, and she conceived and bore Cain, saying, "I have gotten a man with the help of the Lord." And again, she bore his brother Abel. Now Abel was a keeper of sheep, and Cain a worker of the ground. In the course of time Cain brought to the Lord an offering of the fruit of the ground, and Abel also brought of the firstborn of his flock and of their fat portions. And the Lord had regard for Abel and his offering, but for Cain and his offering he had no regard. So Cain was very angry, and his face fell. The Lord said to Cain, "Why are you angry, and why has your face fallen? If you do well, will you not be accepted? And if you do not do well, sin is crouching at the door. Its desire is for you, but you must rule over it."
(Gen 4:1-7ESV)

Hebrew 11:4, says Abel gave his offering by faith. Romans 10:10 declares that faith comes from what we hear. It stands to reason that Cain and Abel could have heard about the role and significance of offering in the prayer process.

THE ORIGIN AND PURPOSE OF PRAYER

Whether they heard it from God or their parents, I cannot tell.

Ever since many factors and dynamics have gone into the prayer process. In my other book, *Understanding the Art of Prayer (Revisited),* under the headings, "Mechanism of prayer, and keys to effective prayer" I explained the different factors and dynamics that go into the prayer process. From the moment you pray, till the answer comes, there are different factors that go into the whole process, which could either work for you or work against you.

LAWS AND PRINCIPLES OF PRAYER

Prayer came about as a result of the structure and order that God established in the beginning between the heavens, and the earth. The structure is that the heavens is God's habitation, while the earth is man's territory or domain.

The order is that God gave humans the right to act on earth, and made us the sole governor of earth affairs. No spirit can act on earth without the cooperation of humans who God put in charge of the earth realm.

From the moment God said in Genesis1:26, "Let us make man in our image, after our likeness. And let them have dominion over the fish of the sea, over the birds of the air, and over the cattle, over all the earth and over every creeping thing on earth." He made mankind the sole governor of earth affairs and excluded himself from the mandate. For this reason, all spirit beings whether the living God or demons must be authorized by humans to act legally on earth, and the only means to achieve that is prayer.

UNDERSTANDING THE CONCEPT OF PRAYER

The Lord retains both the ability to do things and the right to act in heaven. He doesn't need anyone's approval or permission to work in heaven. But on earth, he needs the cooperation of humans to do things.

Prayer is the spiritual bridge that connects the spirit world and the earth. Without it, no one on earth can access the spirit world.

Prayer is the only weapon humans can use to influence both the invisible, and the physical world.

Prayer is the primary means through which humankind either grant or deny spirit beings, whether the living God or Satan, the right to act in the earth realm.

Prayer cuts across all boundaries, be it religion, race, nationality, gender, social class and ranks, geographical location, languages and dialects, and so on.

Prayer is the only means or medium through which God's ability to do things connects with the right of man to act in the world to produce the miraculous and effect changes on earth.

Prayer is you giving God or Satan the right to manifest their power in your life. The spirit you connect with through prayer, controls your life.

And Eli'jah said to Ahab, "Go up, eat and drink; for there is a sound of the rushing of rain." So Ahab went up to eat and to drink. And Eli'jah went up to the top of Carmel; and he bowed himself down upon the earth, and put his face between his knees. And he said to his servant, "Go up now, look toward the sea." And he went up and looked, and said, "There is nothing." And he said, "Go again seven times."

(1 Ki. 18:41-44 RSV)

CHAPTER TWO

5WH PRAYER TECHNIQUE

Having explained how prayer came about, and the main reason we pray, I think it is very important to speak on one of the most effective prayer formulas that you can use to enhance your prayer life. It is a technique that has been used over the years in different field for solving problems, brainstorming, reporting, researching, and even writing. Journalists often use it to gather information about event or incident. Some call it the 5WH technique, method, or formula.

I would like to show you how this formula that people have used in almost all field of works for several years to enhance their activities, can be used to kick-start your prayer life and make it very effective. For the benefit of this teaching, I will call it the "5WH Prayer Technique." It is an easy and very practical way to enhance your prayer life. The method comprises the following:

1. What – this has to do with the things you say when praying
2. Who and whom – the one praying, and the God they pray to
3. Why – speaks of the motive or reason you pray

THE ORIGIN AND PURPOSE OF PRAYER

4. Where – talks about the place you pray
5. When – refers to the time you pray
6. How – deals with the manner or attitude

The Lord Jesus did so many astounding miracles during his earthly ministry. John21:25 says that if every one of them were written, the whole world would not have enough room for the books that would be written. He healed the sick, raised the dead, casted out devils, opened blind eyes and deaf ears, cursed a tree and it withered, cured leprosy, turned water to wine, and he multiplied bread and fish for thousands of people to eat. However, the only thing his disciples ever asked him to teach them how to do, having watched him very closely for about three and a half years was how to pray. This establishes the fact that prayer is taught, and whatever is taught can be learned.

One day Jesus was praying in a certain place. When he finished, one of his disciples said to him, "Lord, teach us to pray, just as John taught his disciples." He said to them, "When you pray, say: "'Father, hallowed be your name, your kingdom come. Give us each day our daily bread. Forgive us our sins, for we also forgive everyone who sins against us. And lead us not into temptation.
(Lk.11:1-4NIV)

Since the Lord Jesus, John the Baptist and the Pharisees taught their respective disciples how to pray, we have to learn from others who are successful in prayer, what they know about the subject. It is important we learn prayer techniques that produce result in order to build an effective and consistent prayer life. What you know about prayer determines the results you produce through it.

5WH PRAYER TECHNIQUE

True knowledge and understanding is required for you to be effective, and consistent in prayer.

WHAT

As earlier mentioned, the "What" constitutes the word content. It is all about the things you say when praying. It is not the amount of time you spend in prayer that determines the quality of your prayer, but what you say when you pray. *We can only talk about what we know.* The knowledge you have about prayer determines what you say, while the things you say determines the result you produce in prayer.

To produce better results, you have to learn what to say when praying. It is not the amount of words you say in prayer that counts, what counts is the quality of words – quality not quantity. There is a way to build your case in prayer that allows you to win. It is a skill you must learn and master in order to produce better results.

A closer look at the Lord's pattern for kingdom prayer highlights the importance of the things we say in prayer. In response to the disciples' request for the Lord Jesus to teach them how to pray, he said in verse 2, "When you pray, say:" I think the reason he said that is because prayer begins with saying something, and what you know about prayer determines what you say. As I said before, a person can only talk about what he or she knows. Prayer becomes fun when you know what to say.

When you pray, don't babble on and on as people of other religions do.

THE ORIGIN AND PURPOSE OF PRAYER

They think their prayers are answered merely by repeating their words again and again. Don't be like them, for your Father knows exactly what you need even before you ask him!
(Matt 6:7-9NLT)

Many spend hours and days praying about a particular thing without receiving answers to their petitions because they merely repeat words, and think God would come through for them because of the amount of time they spend. I'm sorry to announce to you that it doesn't work that way. In the words of Jesus, "When you pray, don't babble on and on as people of other religions do. They think their prayers are answered merely by repeating their words again and again." The only way we can avoid this pitfall in prayer is to learn what to say when praying.

Two men went up to the temple to pray, one a Pharisee and the other a tax collector. The Pharisee stood up and prayed about himself: 'God, I thank you that I am not like other men — robbers, evildoers, adulterers — or even like this tax collector. I fast twice a week and give a tenth of all I get.' "But the tax collector stood at a distance. He would not even look up to heaven, but beat his breast and said, 'God, have mercy on me, a sinner.' "I tell you that this man, rather than the other, went home justified before God. For everyone who exalts himself will be humbled, and he who humbles himself will be exalted.
(Lk.18:10-14NIV)

You'll notice in the above passage that though the two men prayed, only one had positive results. It says both of them went up to the temple to pray, perhaps they spent the same amount of time before God. Nonetheless, only one returned home justified.

5WH PRAYER TECHNIQUE

The passage made it clear that the difference in the result both of them had was determined by what they said when they prayed. It also highlights the kind of attention God gives to what we say when praying. The Lord Jesus said the Pharisee prayed about himself, which means he listened attentively to his prayer and evaluated his word content. While the first spoke about himself, the later pleaded for God's mercy on his life. Apart from their words, the Lord also observed their attitude. I'll speak more on this as we proceed.

I have often heard people say, to be effective in prayer, you have to pray the Scripture. Declare God's word and hold him by his promises. For this reason, when some are praying, they always hold giant print Bible in their hands, thinking God will hear them because they have his words in their hands. Others will open a portion of scripture as they pray and read it aloud. I do not have any problem with these manners of prayer though, all I can say is that the letter kills.

IMPORTANT QUESTIONS

1. Should we pray scripture?
2. If yes, how should we do it?
3. Is it by holding the Bible in your hand when praying?
4. Is it by opening a portion of scripture and reading it loudly?
5. Do I pray scripture by merely quoting Bible verses when praying?

Praying scripture has nothing to do with you opening a portion of Bible passage and reading it aloud.

THE ORIGIN AND PURPOSE OF PRAYER

The letter kills but the Spirit of the word gives life according to the Bible.

He has made us competent as ministers of a new covenant- — not of the letter but of the Spirit; for the letter kills, but the Spirit gives life.
(2 Co.3:6NIV)

To pray scripture means the act of using the truths, principles, and concepts revealed in the written word of God to build your case in a way that gives you advantage in prayer. It is your ability to analyze things in light of scriptures to gain advantage when praying.

A perfect example can be seen in the passage below. It shows how the early church used the truths, and principles of the written word to build their case in prayer in order to move God's hand.

When the apostle Peter and his associate John, went back to the church and reported how the Sanhedrin had threatened and commanded them not to speak or teach at all in the name of Jesus, the brethren raised their voices together in prayer to God, saying:

Sovereign Lord, you made the heaven and the earth and the sea, and everything in them. You spoke by the Holy Spirit through the mouth of your servant, our father David: "'Why do the nations rage and the peoples plot in vain? The kings of the earth take their stand and the rulers gather together against the Lord and against his Anointed One.' Indeed Herod and Pontius Pilate met together with the Gentiles and the people of Israel in this city to conspire against your holy servant Jesus, whom you anointed.

5WH PRAYER TECHNIQUE

They did what your power and will had decided beforehand should happen. Now, Lord, consider their threats and enable your servants to speak your word with great boldness. Stretch out your hand to heal and perform miraculous signs and wonders through the name of your holy servant Jesus." After they prayed, the place where they were meeting was shaken. And they were all filled with the Holy Spirit and spoke the word of God boldly.
(Acts 4:24-31 NIV)

    Let's take a closer look at this passage and examine the way the church first established a connection between their present situations with what king David went through in his days, before using the truths, and principles revealed in the passage they were referring to, to build their case in prayer, which in turn added weight and value to what they said in prayer.

    They started by making reference to what God said in the passage as follows, *"You spoke by the Holy Spirit through the mouth of your servant, our father David"*, knowing that when God speaks, it becomes law. Second, they used the truths revealed in what God said in the passage, through the mouth of King David to lay a foundation on which they built their case by saying, *"Indeed Herod and Pontius Pilate met together with the Gentiles and the people of Israel in this city to conspire against your holy servant Jesus, whom you anointed. They did what your power and will had decided beforehand should happen."*

    When David spoke these words, he didn't only speak about himself. He prophesied about the Christ, who would rule the whole world.

THE ORIGIN AND PURPOSE OF PRAYER

Jesus is the son of David according to the flesh, who was to sit on his throne and rule over the house of Jacob forever (Lk.1:31-33).

Having done that, they stood on it to place a demand for God to act by presenting their request to him in this manner, *"Now, Lord, consider their threats and enable your servants to speak your word with great boldness. Stretch out your hand to heal and perform miraculous signs and wonders through the name of your holy servant Jesus."* By the time they finished prayer, the passage says the place they were meeting was shaken, and they were all filled with the Holy Spirit, and spoke the word of God boldly. Their prayer yielded incredible results.

The reason the early church produced such as amazing results through prayer, is not because they held a big scroll that contains the words of God. It is because they could exegetically interpret scriptures and decode biblical truths, concepts, and principles that they used to establish legal ground on which they stood to provoke the divine release. What they said in prayer was scripturally sound and correct. The result is that they received what they asked God for.

To be effective in prayer, you have to learn what to say. Learning what to say in prayer enhances your prayer life. The easiest way to learn what to say is by listening to those who are effective and consistent in prayer. What you know about prayer determines what you say when praying, which in turn determines the effectiveness and consistency of your prayer life.

5WH PRAYER TECHNIQUE

WHO and WHOM

The "Who" speaks of the one who does the prayer, while the "Whom" represents the God or deity the person prays to. The issue of identity is very important as it relates to prayer. Many don't really know who they are in Christ, and the nature of the God they serve. The revelation knowledge you have about who you are in Christ (divine identity), and the God you serve would make your prayer life effective and consistent.

The book of Matthew16:13-17, recounts how the Lord Jesus asked his disciples this important question about himself. Having revealed the true nature of his person to them for some time, through teaching, preaching, healing and deliverances, the Lord asked them. "Who do men say that I, the Son of Man, am? Some say you are John the Baptist, others say Elijah; and still others say you are Jeremiah or one of the prophets." They replied. "What about you?" Jesus asked them. "Who do you say I am?" Simon Peter answered, "You are the Christ, the Son of the living God."

When the Lord heard the response of the apostle Peter, he said to him, "Blessed are you, Simon son of Jonah, for this was not revealed to you by flesh and blood, but by my Father in heaven." For the Lord Jesus to commend Peter because of the revelation knowledge he had about him, means it is very important. Next, he said to him, "I tell you that you are Peter, and on this rock I will build my church, and the gates of hell shall not prevail against it. I will give you the keys of the kingdom of heaven, and whatever you loose on earth shall be loosed in heaven." Afterward, he commanded his disciples not to tell anyone else that he was the Christ.

THE ORIGIN AND PURPOSE OF PRAYER

Do you see how the revelation knowledge Peter has about Christ gave him advantage over the other disciples? And how he got from the Lord, what the other disciples couldn't receive. The knowledge you have about who you are in Christ, and the God you serve, gives you advantage in prayer.

May grace (God's favor) and peace (which is perfect well-being, all necessary good, all spiritual prosperity, and freedom from fears and agitating passions and moral conflicts) be multiplied to you in [the full, personal, precise, and correct] knowledge of God and of Jesus our Lord. For His divine power has bestowed upon us all things that [are requisite and suited] to life and godliness, through the [full, personal] knowledge of Him Who called us by and to His own glory and excellence (virtue).
(2 Pet.1:2-3 AMP)

The passage above clearly states that God gives us all things that pertain to life and godliness, including abundant grace and peace, through the knowledge we have about him, and his Son Jesus Christ. This suggests that the revelation knowledge you have about God and the Lord Jesus, determines the amount of things that pertain to life and godliness you can enjoy.

There is a portion of scriptures that highlights the important of knowing your position in Christ (your divine identity), and the God you serve. It talks about a group of Jews who went about casting out demons. On one occasion, they tried to use the name of Jesus to drive out evil spirits, saying, "In the name of the Jesus who Paul preaches, I command you to come out." They were the seven sons of Sceva, a Jewish chief priest.

5WH PRAYER TECHNIQUE

The evil spirit they were trying to cast out answered them, "Jesus I know, and I know about Paul, but who are you?" It is so obvious from their declaration that they don't know who they are in Christ, neither do they have a personal relationship with the Lord Jesus like the apostle Paul, since they made reference to the Jesus who Paul preaches. Your identity in Christ makes you unique, it distinguishes you, gives confidence and authority in prayer.

Some Jews who went around driving out evil spirits tried to invoke the name of the Lord Jesus over those who were demon-possessed. They would say, "In the name of Jesus, whom Paul preaches, I command you to come out." Seven sons of Sceva, a Jewish chief priest, were doing this. [One day] the evil spirit answered them, "Jesus I know, and I know about Paul, but who are you?" Then the man who had the evil spirit jumped on them and overpowered them all. He gave them such a beating that they ran out of the house naked and bleeding. (Acts 19:13-16NIV)

Verse 16 informs us that the man who had the evil spirit jumped on them, and overpowered them all. He gave them such a beating that they ran out of the house naked and bleeding. This unfortunate situation happened to the seven sons of Sceva because they don't know who they are, and whose they are.

According Deuteromy32:30, one person is supposed to chase a thousand, and two people ten thousands. But one devil resisted their prayer, and attacked them so aggressively that they ran out of the place bleeding, naked and defeated.

Let me point out here that though they prayed, they didn't produce positive result because of ignorance to their divine identity.

THE ORIGIN AND PURPOSE OF PRAYER

All the demon asked was who they are. Knowing your divine identity and your position in Christ enhances your prayer. If the seven sons of the Jewish high priest, Sceva knew who they were in Christ, they would not have been defeated in prayer, by the devil. Neither would they have spent time in prayer without producing good results.

Just like the sons of Sceva, many people pray today trying to imitate others without producing good results. There is nothing wrong with emulating those who know how to pray effectively. In fact, I encourage people to emulate those who are successful in prayer, with positive fruits that they can point to.

The problem is that no matter how well you try to imitate others, including me, you cannot be effective and consistent until you have a revelation knowledge about your identity in Christ. This is what makes you unique. It sets you apart from the pack, and gives you advantage in prayer. Otherwise, you would pray like many do, but you won't produce good results.

The Lord's pattern for kingdom prayer reveals something very important that I would like to point out from the Scripture below. It highlights the notion of *father and son or daughter relationship.* It begins with, "OUR FATHER IN HEAVEN." This implies that you cannot cultivate a consistent prayer life without a good relationship with God. You cannot live your life the way you want and expect God to answer you when you call (pray).

You need to have a good relationship with the Lord. Accept God's offer for salvation by confessing Jesus as Lord and savior, if you are not born again. Perhaps, you are born again but your life does not glorify God,

5WH PRAYER TECHNIQUE

change your ways and honor God with your life.

Pray then like this: "Our Father in heaven, hallowed be your name. Your kingdom come, your will be done, on earth as it is in heaven. Give us this day our daily bread, and forgive us our debts, as we also have forgiven our debtors. And lead us not into temptation, but deliver us from evil.'
(Matt.6:9-13ESV)

Knowing who you truly are in Christ, and having a comprehensive revelation knowledge about God enhances your prayer life more than anything else, and makes it very effective. As I said before, knowing who you are and whose you are is very important as it concerns prayer.

I encourage you to take some time and ponder these questions. Please be sincere as you meditate, and it will do you good. Who are you in Christ? Do you really have a personal relationship with Jesus? How well do you know the God you serve? Where do you place God in your life? Can you face that situation with confidence and full assurance of faith in Christ, and challenge the devil that is trying to mess-up everything around you? Is your case like that of the sons of Sceva?

Maybe, you go to church, pay your tithes and offerings, pray like everyone else, but you don't have a true relationship with Jesus. It is not too late. You can do it right now regardless of where you are reading this book. If you want to accept Jesus in your life, please pause for a minute and turn to page 167 of this book, under the heading, "Prayer of Salvation." Read through, and make a bold declaration of faith in prayer.

WELCOME BACK!

THE ORIGIN AND PURPOSE OF PRAYER

I would like you to understand that the devil is very sneaky, and would take advantage of you if you don't know who you really are in Christ. The book of Genesis 3:1-5 relates an incident that describes how the devil could manipulate those who are ignorant of their identity.

When God created man in Genesis 1:27, he made him male and female in his own image. Man was created in God's class to be like his maker. Because Eve didn't know she was made like God, Satan took an advantage of her ignorance and made her believe the fruit God asked them not to eat would make her like God.

I know you are saying, "But she didn't need the fruit to make her like God. For she is already like God from the moment she was created." You're perfectly right, and I agree with you. Had she known this simple truth about her identity that is so evident to you and me, Satan would not have had advantage over her.

The Bible declares in Hosea 4:6, "My people are destroyed from lack of knowledge. 'Because you have rejected knowledge, I also reject you from being my priests; because you have ignored the law of your God, I also will ignore your children.'" It takes the revelation knowledge of God's word to lead a victorious Christian life on daily basis.

Now the serpent was more subtle than any other wild creature that the Lord God had made. He said to the woman, "Did God say, 'You shall not eat of any tree of the garden'?" And the woman said to the serpent, "We may eat of the fruit of the trees of the garden; but God said, 'You shall not eat of the fruit of the tree which is in the midst of the garden, neither shall you touch it, lest you die.'"

5WH PRAYER TECHNIQUE

But the serpent said to the woman, "You will not die. For God knows that when you eat of it your eyes will be opened, and you will be like God, knowing good and evil."
(Gen.3:1-5RSV)

Once again, allow me to ask you these simple questions, and please pardon me, if it hurt your feelings. But the reason I am doing it is because of the way it affects the results you produce in prayer. I believe you are reading this book because you want to enhance your prayer life, and produce better results. Whatever is worth doing at all, is worth doing well they say.

On this note, who is Jesus to you? What personal revelation do you have about him? What is your position in Christ? How do you represent him on daily basis? What is the significance of new birth to you? If you can answer all these questions correctly, without a doubt or confusion in your mind, you are on the winning side, and your victory in prayer is certain.

And this is the testimony of John, when the Jews sent priests and Levites from Jerusalem to ask him, "Who are you?" He confessed, and did not deny, but confessed, "I am not the Christ." And they asked him, "What then? Are you Elijah?" He said, "I am not." "Are you the Prophet?" And he answered, "No." So they said to him, "Who are you? We need to give an answer to those who sent us. What do you say about yourself? He said, "I am the voice of one crying out in the wilderness, 'Make straight the way of the Lord,' as the prophet Isaiah said." (Now they had been sent from the Pharisees.) They asked him, "Then why are you baptizing, if you are neither the Christ, nor Elijah, nor the Prophet?" John answered them,

THE ORIGIN AND PURPOSE OF PRAYER

"I baptize with water, but among you stands one you do not know, even he who comes after me, the strap of whose sandal I am not worthy to untie." These things took place in Bethany across the Jordan, where John was baptizing.
(Jn.1:19-28ESV)

The above portion of the Bible further reveals the importance of knowing who you are, more especially in Christ Jesus, the savior of humanity. The Jewish leaders sent the priests and Levites to ask John the Baptist who he was. The reason is because some of the people said John was the Christ, while others claimed he was Elijah. They wanted John to tell them who he was. And because the man knew his identity, he didn't waste any time before revealing to the people who he was.

He started by saying that he wasn't the Christ, for many presumed that he was the Messiah. So, he had to clear that first. For this reason, they asked him, "What then? Are you Elijah? He said, "I am not." "Are you the Prophet?" He answered, "No." Finally they said to him, "Who are you? Give us an answer to take back to those who sent us. What do you say about yourself?"

John replied them in the words of the prophet Isaiah, which God spoke concerning him many years before he was born. "I am the voice of one calling out in the wilderness, 'Make straight the way for the Lord.'"

I like the way John answered them, because of the revelation knowledge he had about his identity, having found his purpose in the Scripture. He discovered his identity in the written word of God, and held to it. He wasn't confused about himself. And he refused to accept what others think and say about him.

5WH PRAYER TECHNIQUE

When the situation resulted in whether or not John had the authority to do what he was doing, the man stood his ground and defended his ministry. He did it because he discovered his identity and purpose in life from the written word of God, and lived by it. There is something written about you in the word of God! Discover it, align your major goals to it, work on it daily, unleash your potential, fulfill your divine purpose and live life to the fullest!

Think of it this way. If a father dies and leaves an inheritance for his young children, those children are not much better off than slaves until they grow up, even though they actually own everything their father had. They have to obey their guardians until they reach whatever age their father set. And that's the way it was with us before Christ came. We were like children; we were slaves to the basic spiritual principles of this world. But when the right time came, God sent his Son, born of a woman, subject to the law. God sent him to buy freedom for us who were slaves to the law, so that he could adopt us as his very own children. And because we are his children, God has sent the Spirit of his Son into our hearts, prompting us to call out, "Abba, Father." Now you are no longer a slave but God's own child. And since you are his child, God has made you his heir.
(Gal. 4:1-7NLT)

The passage above shows that as long as the heir, who by virtue of birth and according to law, owns everything in the house, remains a child, he is not different from a servant. The heir is subject to custodians who tell him how to live his life.

He could be manipulated, abused or denied his privileges until he comes to the knowledge of who he really is and his position in the house.

THE ORIGIN AND PURPOSE OF PRAYER

If he doesn't know the true identity of his father, what the father kept for him, his position, rights and privileges in the house as the heir, a servant that is supposed to attend him, could order him around. Don't let this be your case!

In summary, to gain advantage in prayer, you need a revelation knowledge of God's word about your divine identity, position, rights and privileges, who your father is, how he works and what he does. Knowing who you are, and whose you are would cause your enemies to tremble before you.

The "Who and Whom", which revolves around identity, whether that of the person who prays or the God he prays to, is centered on revelation knowledge. That is to say, the knowledge you have about yourself in light of the written word, and the one you have about God give you an edge in prayer.

WHY

This has to do with the reason, motive, or basis that causes you to pray the way you do. It is the reason behind your motivation, and since there could be no motivation without a motive, God judges the motive not the action. Wrong motive causes wicked action, while good motive leads to noble act.

When the motive is erroneous, our prayers won't produce positive results regardless of how long we pray. It is good to emulate those who have succeeded in prayer, but before you do what they are doing, try to find out what gives them the right to say and do whatever they do in prayer.

5WH PRAYER TECHNIQUE

To illustrate my point, I would like to share something that happened one day at our church. My pastor and spiritual father, the apostle Michael Adeyemi Adefarasin who is known worldwide as a man of strategic prayer, did something one day that surprised me.

It is about someone who the enemy terribly attacked with a very serious sickness. My pastor stood in prayer and said, "Lord, I divert the arrows that have been shot against this person to myself." Almost everyone who heard him that day, including me would have said in their mind, "How dare you make such prayers, considering the critical condition of the person, and not knowing the nature of arrows that the wicked shot." There were trains of thoughts in my mind as I tried to figure out what could have given him the audacity to make such prayer.

At a time I asked myself whether he had any knowledge of the person's secret deeds that resulted in such situation. Why would somebody want to carry the consequences of someone else's wicked acts on his head? I muttered. It was something I could not understand at the time.

There is no doubt my pastor had reasons for his action. He probably knew something that gave him the boldness to engage the enemies the way he did. If not, he wouldn't have done it. Nonetheless, for anybody to go out like the sons of Sceva, and imitate my pastor by trying to divert the arrows that the enemy shot at someone else, simply because he heard or saw him do it, would be a fatal or catastrophic error. Because he or she may not wakeup to see the next day. This may sound funny to some, but it is the fact.

THE ORIGIN AND PURPOSE OF PRAYER

The reason I decided to tell the story is to show you why some people fall in the battlefield, and become the victim rather than being the victor. The enemy is not as powerful as some think, but our ignorance is what gives them the upper hand over us in battle. Don't do things because someone else does it. Even if you have to do what others are doing, since we learn from people, please try and find out why they do whatever they are doing so you don't become a prey to your enemy. People who do astonishing things in prayer, like my pastor, have a revelation knowledge about what they are doing that gives them the courage to engage the enemy the way they do.

When the apostle Paul casted out devils, he had a revelation knowledge about his action that allowed him to win, as we observe in the words of the demon, "*Jesus I know, and I know about Paul, but who are you?*" Satan knew Paul had reasons to say, and do what he did to him, but not everyone has that right. It is very important to know the things that give you the right to take certain actions.

What you know becomes the motive behind your action, and when you act in this manner, you would have something to point to as a reference that authorizes you to do whatever you are doing. Such knowledge gives you confidence, audacity, boldness, self-assurance, and passion to undertake some course of actions that others may never attempt.

The reason (why) is very important because God judges our motives not the actions. 1Samuel16:7, says humans focus on the outward appearance, but God looks at the heart. While men applaud our actions, God judges our intention.

5WH PRAYER TECHNIQUE

And when the motive is erroneous, he won't grant it no matter how much we pray about it.

The Bible passage below says the reason we don't have what we want is because we fail to ask God for it, and even when we make effort to ask, we don't receive because we have wrong motives. The "Why" is very essential in prayer, and when you get it right, every other thing will fall in line. When God who judges intention, approves of your actions, no devil can resist you.

You want what you don't have, so you scheme and kill to get it. You are jealous of what others have, but you can't get it, so you fight and wage war to take it away from them. Yet you don't have what you want because you don't ask God for it. And even when you ask, you don't get it because your motives are all wrong—you want only what will give you pleasure.
(Jas 4:2-3NLT)

I like the portion of scriptures below, as it further explains the importance of having the right reason and standing on it to ask God for things in time of need. The Lord Jesus asked the Father to glorify him with the glory he had with him before the world begun. Nonetheless, before he made the request, he first spoke about how he glorified the Father on the earth, in that he accomplished the work he gave him to do. So, based on what he did for the Father's honor, he demanded a remuneration for the work well-done.

The promise God the Father made to him, and the task he gave him to do, which he did and finished became the reason he demanded what he asked of the Father.

THE ORIGIN AND PURPOSE OF PRAYER

He didn't go before the Father and say, "Father, you are a good God, and I am your son, give me the glory I had with you before the world begun. So that everyone will know and believe that I am your son." There is a protocol that has to be properly observed as it relates to prayer. The knowledge and understanding you have about this procedure would determine the effectiveness of your prayers.

When Jesus had spoken these words, he lifted up his eyes to heaven, and said, "Father, the hour has come; glorify your Son that the Son may glorify you, since you have given him authority over all flesh, to give eternal life to all whom you have given him. And this is eternal life, that they know you the only true God, and Jesus Christ whom you have sent. I glorified you on earth, having accomplished the work that you gave me to do. And now, Father, glorify me in your own presence with the glory that I had with you before the world existed. (Jn.17:1-5ESV)

Pay the price and you will get the prize! Another person who did almost what the Lord Jesus did in the above scripture is King Hezekiah. The Bible tells us that the king Hezekiah was seriously sick and was at the point of death when the major prophet Isaiah, the son of Amoz came to him and said, "This is what the Lord says: 'Put your house in order, because you are going to die; you will not recover.'"

When the king heard this, he turned his face to the wall and prayed to the Lord saying, "Remember, O Lord, how I have walked before you faithfully and with a wholehearted devotion and have done what is good in your eyes." Then he broke down and wept bitterly.

5WH PRAYER TECHNIQUE

Immediately, according to verse 4, the Lord spoke to the prophet Isaiah, "Go back to Hezekiah and tell him, 'this is what the Lord, the God of your father David, says: I have heard your prayer and seen your tears; I will add fifteen years to your life. And I will deliver you and this city from the hand of the king of Assyria. I will defend this city." In addition, the prophet gave him a sign from the Lord to confirm his word by making the sun's shadow to move ten steps backward on the sundial of Ahaz.

Prayer works wonders for those who know how to pray effectively! The king Hezekiah used it to force God to change his death verdict that was pronounced against him, through the great prophet Isaiah and turned it into a blessing. Furthermore, he got his healing, had fifteen more years added to his life. God also promised to deliver the city and gave him a sign to confirm his word.

This whole thing happened because the king put forth his case, and reminded God all the sacrifices he made to honor his name. And since he found good reasons, God changed his mind from killing him, and blessed him instead.

In those days Hezekiah became ill and was at the point of death. The prophet Isaiah son of Amoz went to him and said, "This is what the Lord says: Put your house in order, because you are going to die; you will not recover." Hezekiah turned his face to the wall and prayed to the Lord, "Remember, O Lord, how I have walked before you faithfully and with wholehearted devotion and have done what is good in your eyes." And Hezekiah wept bitterly. Then the word of the Lord came to Isaiah: "Go and tell Hezekiah, 'This is what the Lord, the God of your father David, says: I have heard your prayer and seen your tears; I will add fifteen years to your life.

THE ORIGIN AND PURPOSE OF PRAYER

And I will deliver you and this city from the hand of the king of Assyria. I will defend this city. "'This is the Lord's sign to you that the Lord will do what he has promised: I will make the shadow cast by the sun go back the ten steps it has gone down on the stairway of Ahaz.'" So the sunlight went back the ten steps it had gone down.
(Is. 38:1-8 NIV)

This reminds me of the promises God made to me some time ago, when I fasted and prayed for about one thousand three hundred and sixty days (1,360), eating once a day. I gave a detail explanation of this experience in my other book, *Understanding the Art of Prayer (Revisited)*, in chapter seven, under the heading, "Fasting." For more information on this, please go to the book.

Since I finished what he asked me to do at the time, each time I face challenging situations that demand I make reference to that very promise in prayer, it becomes a legal ground on which I build and argue my case. Knowing also that God keeps covenant, and whenever he speaks, it becomes law, gives me the audacity to engage in certain things especially in prayer.

This is why I often tell those who take classes on prayer with me that before they do whatever they see me do, they should try and find out what gives me the courage to take the action. Otherwise, they may do the same thing but not have the same results.

For this reason, I try as much as I can to share my personal experiences with those around me, so as to let them know some of the things we did that brought us to where we are now. And how we use some of those things to gain advantage over the enemies in prayer.

5WH PRAYER TECHNIQUE

The Lord said through the mouth of the prophet Isaiah that you need to remind him of certain things, and build your case with those evidence that give you superiority of means in prayer, so that you can be vindicated or proved right when you present your argument before the heavenly courtroom.

Put Me in remembrance [remind Me of your merits]; let us plead and argue together. Set forth your case, that you may be justified (proved right).
(Is.43:26AMP)

This is one of the reasons we teach about prayer. It is a hard work and discipline that demands a lot of sacrifices for it to produce the desired results. The Lord Jesus taught prayer, John the Baptist also taught his disciples about prayer, because the knowledge you have about the subject determines the consistency of your prayer life.

You have to learn the prayer techniques that work from those who have practiced it over the years and produced consistent results. Since prayer can be taught, there should be schools of prayer, where people can learn how to be more effective and consistent in their prayer life.

From the little I have written and shared on the subject of prayer, I believe you'll all agree with me that God gave me special grace for strategic prayer. It is my strength zone, and one of my areas of excellence. Prayer is one of the things I am most passionate about. Something I like to talk about, and do whenever I have the opportunity.

THE ORIGIN AND PURPOSE OF PRAYER

Based on several years of experience in the field of prayer, the Lord gave me the grace to write an intensive prayer-teaching course on the Art of Prayer, that I use in teaching and training people. The course comprises three levels. First, is the Preliminary, also known as Class 101. Second, is Intermediate, also called Class 201. Third, is "Advanced Level," and it consists of four sections namely Classes 301, 401, 501 and 601.

We have used this course to train intercessors and prayer warriors to be more effective and consistent in prayer. Another good thing about it is that it can be used by churches, Bible institutes or seminaries, ministries and so on to teach people about prayer. Some use the course as handouts, and my books as textbooks to teach on prayer.

1john1:1, says that which was from the beginning, that we have seen and heard, saw with our eyes and touched with our hands concerning the word of life, is what we proclaim to you. The apostle John wasn't just recounting a story he heard from someone else. He spoke about the thing he has seen and heard, saw with his eyes and touched with his hands, which means he had the experience, knowledge, understanding and authority to speak on the subject.

As far as prayer is concerned, by the grace of God, we have the knowledge and understanding, experience, expertise, discipline, grace, and the authority to do what we are doing. We served as the national prayer director for Action Chapel International (ACI) Benin, and also the leader of intercessory group for nine years.

5WH PRAYER TECHNIQUE

Action Chapel International is founded by the archbishop Nicholas Duncan-Williams, who is known worldwide as the apostle of strategic prayers. In addition, we organized and led prayer for the apostle Michael Adeyemi Adefarasin, who is also known worldwide as a man of strategic prayers. We also taught, and directed prayers at different places for several years. Prayer is something we have experienced in words and deeds for many years.

After the Lord had finished speaking to Job, he said to Eliphaz the Temanite: "I am angry with you and your two friends, for you have not spoken accurately about me, as my servant Job has. So take seven bulls and seven rams and go to my servant Job and offer a burnt offering for yourselves. My servant Job will pray for you, and I will accept his prayer on your behalf. I will not treat you as you deserve, for you have not spoken accurately about me, as my servant Job has." So Eliphaz the Temanite, Bildad the Shuhite, and Zophar the Naamathite did as the Lord commanded them, and the Lord accepted Job's prayer. (Job 42:7-9NLT)

From what the Bible tells us about Job, we saw all that he went through due to satanic attacks and orchestrations. Before Satan got the right or permission from God to carry out his atrocities against Job, he was commended and much-admired by the Lord because of his personal integrity and the manner he walked before him.

The Bible informs us that his sons normally take turns to hold feasts in their homes, and they would invites their three sisters to celebrate with them.

THE ORIGIN AND PURPOSE OF PRAYER

When the feasting had ended, Job would get up early in the morning and offered a burnt offering for each of them. He did this regularly because he felt his children might have sinned and cursed God in their hearts.

When God finally visited Job, after his trial ended, he commanded Eliphaz the Temanite, Bildad the Shuhite, and Zophar the Naamathite to take seven bulls and seven rams to his servant Job for a burnt offering because he was angry with them for the way them spoke about him.

Take seven bulls and seven rams and go to my servant Job and offer a burnt offering for yourselves. My servant Job will pray for you, and I will accept his prayer on your behalf. I will not treat you as you deserve, for you have not spoken accurately about me, as my servant Job has." So Eliphaz the Temanite, Bildad the Shuhite, and Zophar the Naamathite did as the Lord commanded them, and the Lord accepted Job's prayer.

The man Job had something that his three friends didn't have, which later gave him an edge over them. He had a covenant of answered prayer with God that distinguished him from his friends. God himself testified in verse 8 that he will accept Job's prayer on behalf of his friends and do them good for his sake.

God also called Job his servant even though the Scriptures didn't points out clearly the nature of services he was rendering to God. But from the look of things, it appears he was called to stand in the gap for others, before the Lord and plead their cause. Based on this little advantage Job had with God, he could pray for anyone at any time, and the Lord would grant his requests.

5WH PRAYER TECHNIQUE

Have you got enough "Why" to engage in that prayer, and change that situation in your life and family? If yes, arise and act!

WHERE

The "Where" has to do with the location (place) we make our prayers. It is very important to know how location can affect the effectiveness of your prayers. The ability to exercise divine authority, because of the finished work of Christ has been given to us but we do not have the right to exercise it everywhere, because the latter is geographical.

Everyone has a sphere of influence where they can freely exercise their right to do things without any resistance or opposition. Many Christians have often fallen into this error because once they get born again, they think they can move freely from one region to another, and engage whatever they find on the way in fierce battle. The truth is that most of the people who do this, come back with a lot of complaints about different kinds of attack both spiritual and physical.

As earlier mentioned, we may have the ability to do things (power) at any time, but not the right to act (authority) in all places, because the latter is geographically bestowed by those who have the right to act in that particular area.

First, you must ask yourself whether you have the right to do whatever you want to do in prayer at the place you are, before you start. You may have the power to do whatever you have in mind to do at any time because of the finished work of Christ on the cross for you, but having the right to act in that location is another thing.

THE ORIGIN AND PURPOSE OF PRAYER

Or else, your action could be questioned. This is why some face attack and suffer demonic aggression after doing some prayers.

Let me use our local churches for example. No matter how powerful a servant of God may be, he cannot move to another person's chapel to do whatever he has been called and sent by God to do, without been invited. But when another minister invites him to preach in their church, the right to act that those who invite him have is legally conferred on him by the simple act of invitation, so that whatever he does in that church is legal since those in charge of the place endorse it.

That is to say, whenever a resident or host pastor, invites a guest minister, what he actually does by the simple act of inviting the other minister is to grant them the right to exercise their power (anointing) within their space. This is why in most cases, when the guest speaker comes, the host minister introduces him to his congregation and tells him things like, "Be free to do whatever God puts in your mind for my people." Once this is done and all protocols is duly observed, the host minister officially cedes his right to act by virtue of his position in that particular jurisdiction (chapel) to the guest minister.

On the other hand, if the minister thinks because he is famous, decides to come to your church without been invited by those in authority at your sanctuary, walks to the altar, takes the microphones and start preaching, simply because he has a mega church and thousands of members, the least member of your church would question his right to act, and he would be humiliated regardless of his anointing, position and fame.

5WH PRAYER TECHNIQUE

Just as it is with the local church, the same applies to the hospital, prison, family house and home town. There are people placed in authority at these different places, who retain the right to act, and whose actions cannot be question or undermined whenever they act.

I have seen many instance when a newly born again Christian, pushed with zeal without knowledge goes to his family house to destroy their family altar, and how it always result in continuous combat as those in authority at the place join forces to fetch out and hunt the Christian down through enchantment, divination, witchcraft, incantation, sacrifices and so on, until they finally destroy the person for their action.

To destroy a family evil altar is a noble act from Biblical point of view. However, the elders of the family who are not Christian like you, hold a different point of view and they would use all means at their disposal to fight you in an effort to preserve the family heritage.

In this case, the proper way to go about it is to share your plans with those in authority (those who have the right of words) in the family who share your faith. They may not know how to execute the plan, but when they support you, and take the lead, they will call on you to go ahead and carry out the action in their presence. By so doing, they conferred on you the right to act (authority), by virtue of their position in the family, and when attacks come from those who oppose the action, they will stand and defend you.

THE ORIGIN AND PURPOSE OF PRAYER

Before you go ahead with that prison, hospital or whatever ministry God has called you to, first get a way to meet with those in authority at the different place you intend going for ministration to learn about their procedure. Second, talk with other known ministers who are doing the same work at the place and find out from them, how they started, the challenges they encountered at the beginning, how they overcame and what has kept them going in spite of whatever that might have come their way. If possible, let them introduce you to the people at the place. That would make things easier for you to start fulfilling your divine mandate. There is a proper way to go about things, find it out and follow the procedure. You will be glad you did!

They went across the lake to the region of the Gerasenes. When Jesus got out of the boat, a man with an evil spirit came from the tombs to meet him.. This man lived in the tombs, and no one could bind him any more, not even with a chain. For he had often been chained hand and foot, but he tore the chains apart and broke the irons on his feet. No one was strong enough to subdue him. Night and day among the tombs and in the hills he would cry out and cut himself with stones. When he saw Jesus from a distance, he ran and fell on his knees in front of him. He shouted at the top of his voice, "What do you want with me, Jesus, Son of the Most High God? Swear to God that you won't torture me!" For Jesus had said to him, "Come out of this man, you evil spirit!" Then Jesus asked him, "What is your name?" "My name is Legion," he replied, "for we are many." And he begged Jesus again and again not to send them out of the area. A large herd of pigs was feeding on the nearby hillside. The demons begged Jesus, "Send us among the pigs; allow us to go into them."

5WH PRAYER TECHNIQUE

He gave them permission, and the evil spirits came out and went into the pigs. The herd, about two thousand in number, rushed down the steep bank into the lake and were drowned.
(Mk.5:1-13NIV)

This portion of scriptures show us how the Lord Jesus crossed the lake to the region of the Gerasenes for a special mission. On their arrival, a man possessed by an evil spirit came out of the cemetery to meet him. The man lived in the tombs, and no one could bind him anymore, not even with chains. Because whenever they bound him with shackles and chains, he would tear the chains apart, and break the shackles in pieces. No one was strong enough to subdue him.

When he saw Jesus from afar, he ran and fell down before him. The evil spirit begged Jesus not to torture him, and when the Lord commanded the unclean spirit to come out of the man, the spirit earnestly pleaded with the Lord and begged him again not to send them out of the area. They even asked him the permission to live in the pigs that were feeding nearby, rather than to be driven out of the zone.

The demons did this because they knew that the right to act at any place is regional. They preferred to remain within that locality where they had the legal right to carry out their activities than be driven to an unknown territory, where they may not be given such right by those living there.

In my other book, *Strategic Prayer,* under the heading "Binding the Strongman,"

THE ORIGIN AND PURPOSE OF PRAYER

I explained how the demons earnestly begged the Lord Jesus not to send them out of the area when he commanded the spirits to leave the man because the territory was their home and jurisdiction. They even preferred to live in pigs than to be driven out of the region.

Demons are territorial, because their power is regional, and it is determined by the authority the people living in the area give them through certain practices, customs, systems, words, and deeds that open doors and establish legal grounds in the spirit realms for them to operate. So, driving them out of the region terminates their authority and operation because it causes them to lose the legitimate right to function in the new territory that those living there may not do any of the things that give them the authority to operate.

As soon as the Lord granted them the permission to enter the pigs, scriptures say they went out of the man immediately and entered the animals. But I love what the pigs did. The whole herd of about two thousand in number, rushed down the steep bank into the lake and drowned in the water.

It is as if those pigs said to one another, though humans might have given these demons the right to operate in this region, we would rather die than allow them use our body as instrument. Perhaps, they saw what the demons did to the man they had previously possessed and how they almost destroy his life in that, they separated him from other people, made him dwell in the tombs, caused him to cut himself with sharp stones and cry with a loud voice day and night as he wandered in the mountains and graveyard.

5WH PRAYER TECHNIQUE

Come to think about it, if the pigs, as dirty as they are, would rather preferred to die than allow evil spirits use their body as instrument to carryout demonic activities, why would you who God created in his image and likeness for a unique assignment on earth, yield your beautiful body to Satan as instrument that he willingly uses to destroy lives and destinies?

This is very sad! If God has ministered to you through this word, and you have the impression that Satan is using your body to advance his agenda, you can liberate yourself right now. Just make this declaration after me, as I join my voice and faith to yours in prayer.

Dear Lord, I thank you for your mercy toward me. Your word declares that it is not of him who wills, nor of him who runs, but God who shows mercy (Rom.9:16). In whatever way I have yielded my life and body to the wicked as instrument of destruction, I repent, renounce and terminate such act.

In the name of Jesus, I break every covenant that exists between me and demonic spirit. I set myself free from their grips, by the power of the Holy Spirit. I decree and declare that my body is the temple of the Spirit of God. Therefore, Satan I command you by divine authority to take your hands off my life. In Jesus mighty name! Amen!

Congratulations!

Beginning today, may you enjoy total freedom and peace from demonic assault, and manipulation in any area of your life that has been under the influence of negative forces. I decree, and declare that your deliverance is permanent. In Jesus mighty name. Amen!

THE ORIGIN AND PURPOSE OF PRAYER

All we are trying to show you through these different passages in the Bible is the importance of knowing whether or not you have the authority to do the thing you want to do at the very place you're planning to do them. So that you don't make the same mistakes that most people make in their daily Christian walk. My desire is to see you walk in victory on daily basis.

There were times we missed it, but the good thing is the special grace God gave me to always learn from my errors and use my experiences to admonish others, so they don't make the same mistakes.

That night the Lord said to him, "Take your father's bull, and the second bull seven years old, and pull down the altar of Baal that your father has, and cut down the Asherah that is beside it and build an altar to the Lord your God on the top of the stronghold here, with stones laid in due order. Then take the second bull and offer it as a burnt offering with the wood of the Asherah that you shall cut down." So Gideon took ten men of his servants and did as the Lord had told him. But because he was too afraid of his family and the men of the town to do it by day, he did it by night. When the men of the town rose early in the morning, behold, the altar of Baal was broken down, and the Asherah beside it was cut down, and the second bull was offered on the altar that had been built. And they said to one another, "Who has done this thing?" And after they had searched and inquired, they said, "Gideon the son of Joash has done this thing." Then the men of the town said to Joash, "Bring out your son, that he may die, for he has broken down the altar of Baal and cut down the Asherah beside it." But Joash said to all who stood against him, "Will you contend for Baal? Or will you save him?

5WH PRAYER TECHNIQUE

Whoever contends for him shall be put to death by morning. If he is a god, let him contend for himself, because his altar has been broken down." Therefore on that day Gideon was called Jerubbaal, that is to say, "Let Baal contend against him," because he broke down his altar. (Judg. 6:25-32ESV)

The above passage relates how Gideon pulled down the altar of Baal in his father's house following the instruction the angel of the Lord gave him. However, he had to do it at night because he was afraid of his family members and the men of the town.

When the people of the city rose early in the morning, they noticed that the altar of Baal was broken. The first question they asked is, "Who has done this thing?" Second, they opened an investigation to know whether the one who did it has the right to do what he did. Third, when they found out that Gideon broke the altar of Baal, they asked his father to bring him out so they could kill him.

One of my friends always says, "For every action of God, there is a corresponding demonic reaction." Gideon did what God asked him to do, but the enemies came after him in an attempt to destroy his life. His action, which was divinely inspired, provoked a demonic reaction that almost ended his life. Had Gideon's father, who was a man in authority at the time, not spoken in his defense, and delivered him from death, he would have died for his action.

The truth is that Gideon has the ability to carry out the action, but not the right to do it. Some may have the right, and not have the ability, while others may have the ability, but not have the right.

To be on the safe side, I recommend you ask yourself both questions. Check whether you have the power, and authority before you act.

Don't go everywhere exercising your divine authority without first seeking the right to act from those in authority at the place where you live or wherever you desire to exercise your gifts. Before you begin that prison or hospital ministry, please use wisdom like Gideon did, and save yourself the trouble of being frustrated, disappointed, embarrassed or shamed. Find out the best approach and duly respect the procedure put in place by those in charge, and make sure you obtain appropriate authorization from the right source, so you don't give the enemy an occasion to resist, attack, humiliate or discredit you.

WHEN

The "When" has to do with divine timing. It is very important we understand how God works in order not to miss out on his plans. Whatever God does, he does it at his own time. Understanding divine timing is key to effective prayers, because it allows you to decode what God is getting ready to do, so you can position yourself in prayer and birth it on earth.

The Bible declares in Ecl.3:1, that there is a time for everything, and a season for every activity under heaven. Verse 11 says he makes all things beautiful in its time. To be effective in prayer, you have to be sensitive to divine timing. God does things according to his calendar not yours.

5WH PRAYER TECHNIQUE

Those who understand divine timing, always produce better results in prayer, because they know what to do, and are able to device suitable course of action for the occasion.

In his devotional, The Lamp, (23rd edition), under the heading, "Understanding the Times 3", my papa the archbishop Duncan-Williams writes, "As children of God we must know how to operate with God's time. It is only then that we will be able to receive all we need at the time expected. The world operates on time. Every activity goes with time. In the same way God operates with time. It is very important to note that God wants us to know what time it is in order to take a stand."

The book of 1Chronicles12:32 explains how the understanding the tribe of Issachar had about times and seasons, gave them superiority of means over their brethren. And because of this unique ability that they had, even though they were few in number when compared to other tribes, they produced about two hundred leaders that gave their relatives instructions on what to do, and the best course of action to take. In the end, they became commanders over their relatives.

Of Issachar, men who had understanding of the times, to know what Israel ought to do, 200 chiefs, and all their kinsmen under their command.
(1Chro. 12:32ESV)

As soon as God anointed David king over his people Israel, the Philistines heard about it, and mobilized all their forces to capture him. I supposed they did this because of what David had done to one of their champions,

THE ORIGIN AND PURPOSE OF PRAYER

named Goliath from Gath and other Philistine military commanders who David and his mighty men killed during their military campaigns (1Sam.17:41-54, 18:13-16).

They might have seen the occasion as payback time to avenge the death of their army commanders, and soldiers that David destroyed in war, since he now reign over Israel in place of King Saul. When David heard they were coming against him, he deployed his mighty men, and went out to meet them.

The Philistines had invaded the valley of Rephaim to provoke King David to war. But before David engaged them in battle, he first inquired of the Lord, "Should I go out to fight the Philistines? Will you deliver them into my hands?" In response, the Lord said, "Yes, go ahead. I will deliver them into your hands." So David and his men of war went to Baal Perazim and defeated the philistines there. "God did it!" David Exclaimed. "He used me to burst through my enemies like a raging flood!" So they named that place Baal-perazim.

When the Philistines heard that David had been anointed king over all Israel, they mobilized all their forces to capture him. But David was told they were coming, so he marched out to meet them. The Philistines arrived and made a raid in the valley of Rephaim. So David asked God, "Should I go out to fight the Philistines? Will you hand them over to me?" The Lord replied, "Yes, go ahead. I will hand them over to you." So David and his troops went up to Baal-perazim and defeated the Philistines there. "God did it!" David exclaimed. "He used me to burst through my enemies like a raging flood!" So they named that place Baal-perazim (which means "the Lord who bursts through").

5WH PRAYER TECHNIQUE

The Philistines had abandoned their gods there, so David gave orders to burn them. But after a while the Philistines returned and raided the valley again. And once again David asked God what to do. "Do not attack them straight on," God replied. "Instead, circle around behind and attack them near the poplar trees.

When you hear a sound like marching feet in the tops of the poplar trees, go out and attack! That will be the signal that God is moving ahead of you to strike down the Philistine army." So David did what God commanded, and they struck down the Philistine army all the way from Gibeon to Gezer. So David's fame spread everywhere, and the Lord caused all the nations to fear David.
(1Chro. 14:8-17NLT)

Once again, the Philistines attacked the people in the valley to provoke David and his troops to a fight. David again inquired of the Lord. God told him not to go directly after them. Instead, he asked him to circle around and attacked them from behind, near the poplar trees.

In addition, the Lord asked him to wait until he hears a sound like marching feet in the tops of the poplar tree, before he goes out and attack. For that would be a sign that God has gone ahead of him to strike down the Philistine army. David did as God commanded him, and they struck down the Philistines army from Gibeon to Gazer. Then David's fame spread everywhere, and the Lord caused all the nations to fear him.

I mentioned in my previous book, *Understanding the Art of Prayer (Revisited),* that king David's victory was due to his ability to inquire of the Lord for direction and his obedience to divine instruction.

THE ORIGIN AND PURPOSE OF PRAYER

God commanded him to wait until he hears the sound of matching feet in the tops of the trees before going out to attack his enemies, and he did. Had he gone out to attack the Philistines before the appointed time, he would have faced them alone and lost the battle, because God would not have gone with him to the battlefield.

The Bible declares in Psalm 102:13 that God will arise and have compassion on Zion because the set time to favor her, the appointed time, has come. According to Ecclesiastes 9:11, the race is not to the swift or the battle to the strong, nor does food come to the wise or wealth to the brilliant or favor to the learned, but time and chances happen to them all. Those who are sensitive to divine timing always produce incredible results through prayer.

This is what the Lord Almighty, the God of Israel, says to all those I carried into exile from Jerusalem to Babylon: "Build houses and settle down; plant gardens and eat what they produce. Marry and have sons and daughters; find wives for your sons and give your daughters in marriage, so that they too may have sons and daughters. Increase in number there; do not decrease. Also, seek the peace and prosperity of the city to which I have carried you into exile. Pray to the Lord for it, because if it prospers, you too will prosper." Yes, this is what the Lord Almighty, the God of Israel, says: "Do not let the prophets and diviners among you deceive you. Do not listen to the dreams you encourage them to have. They are prophesying lies to you in my name. I have not sent them," declares the Lord. This is what the Lord says: "When seventy years are completed for Babylon, I will come to you and fulfill my gracious promise to bring you back to this place. For I know the plans I have for you," declares the Lord, "plans to prosper you and not to harm you, plans to give you hope and a future.

5WH PRAYER TECHNIQUE

Then you will call upon me and come and pray to me, and I will listen to you. You will seek me and find me when you seek me with all your heart. I will be found by you," declares the Lord, "and will bring you back from captivity. I will gather you from all the nations and places where I have banished you," declares the Lord, "and will bring you back to the place from which I carried you into exile."
(Jer. 29:4-14NIV)

The passage above places more emphasis on the significance of divine timing and how it affects our prayers. When the people of God went to exile from Jerusalem to Babylon as punishment for their wicked practices and disobedience to God's commandment, some thought they could return home anytime soon.

God had to make them understand by the letter the prophet Jeremiah sent them that no amount of prayers or sacrifices would make him change his mind about their return from exile before the seventy years he assigned them. His plan was when seventy years were completed in Babylon, he would visit them and fulfill his gracious promise to bring them back to their home land. "Then you will call upon me and come and pray to me, and I will listen to you. You will seek me and find me when you seek me with all your heart. I will be found by you and will bring you back from captivity," declares the Lord.

To be very effective, and consistent in prayer, you need to understand divine timing. God is sovereign, he does whatever he chooses at his own time. He will not do anything that contradicts his word and principles.

THE ORIGIN AND PURPOSE OF PRAYER

Learn more about his ways and will, from the written word. The knowledge you have about how God works, and when he does things enhances your prayer life.

HOW

The "How" has to do with the skill and expertise needed for effective and consistent prayer. It is a discipline that must be learned in order to produce better results.

When the disciples saw the way the Lord Jesus prayed, they asked him to teach them how to pray, as John taught his disciples. There was something Jesus knew about the subject that his disciples needed to learn before they can have the kind of results that Jesus himself produced. The fact Jesus, and John taught their respective disciples how to pray, is an indication that it can be learned (if it can be taught, it can be learned). As earlier stated, you learn the "how-to" through study, practice, or observation.

The Lord Jesus used the teaching to explain the right manner and attitude for effective prayers. It shows how certain things are more important than the others in prayer, to help you put first thing first (prioritized), and pray orderly. The whole thing is about learning what works in prayer and applying them. It helps you to know what to say, why say it, when to say it, and where to say it.

He was praying in a certain place, and when he ceased, one of his disciples said to him, "Lord, teach us to pray, as John taught his disciples." And he said to them, "When you pray, say: "Father, hallowed be thy name.

5WH PRAYER TECHNIQUE

Thy kingdom come. Give us each day our daily bread; and forgive us our sins, for we ourselves forgive every one who is indebted to us; and lead us not into temptation."
(Lk.11:1-4RSV)

The teaching of the Lord begins with, "When you pray, not if you pray." Prayer is a necessity! It is mankind giving God the permission to interfere in earth affairs, says Dr. Myles. Prayer demands a lot of discipline, sacrifices, learning and practices to produce consistent results. Once acquired, the skill must be continually worked on to ensure effective and constant results.

While speaking on the "What" formula, I explained how the early church leaders skillfully used the written word of God to build their case in prayer, in times of trouble, and moved the mighty hand of God to action on their behalf. We saw how they first established a link between what they were going through at the time with what happened in the days of their ancestor, king David, before using the truths, and principles revealed in the passage they were referring to, to build their case in prayer.

To do this successfully, you have to acquire the skill through study, practice and observation. Learn how to use scriptures in prayer to establish legal grounds, make connections, gain advantage, move the hand of God to action and obtain your desires.

When the church finished praying in the passage we read, the place they were meeting was shaken, and they were all filled with the Holy Spirit, and spoke the word of God with boldness because of how they intelligently, and strategically used scriptures in prayer to gain advantage and obtain their requests (Acts4:23-31).

THE ORIGIN AND PURPOSE OF PRAYER

Every successful intercessor and prayer warrior understands this technique and often uses it in prayer to gain ground, and achieve incredible results. A very good example is the great prophet Moses, who is considered by many as one of the greatest intercessor that ever lived. He was so skilled in the art that every time he stands in prayer for the people of Israel before God, he wins and causes the people to triumph regardless of the charges that are leveled against them, whether by God or humans.

His incontestable expertise in the field of intercession remains a point of reference till today because of the number of positive results he produced through prayer, notably at the time when it appeared impossible. He was able to overturn negative verdict, reverse curses, stop imminent destruction, block aggression, appease God's anger and force his hand to action on behalf of his people through the power of prayer, by using this method.

"I have seen these people," the Lord said to Moses, "and they are a stiff-necked people. Now leave me alone so that my anger may burn against them and that I may destroy them. Then I will make you into a great nation." But Moses sought the favor of the Lord his God. "O Lord," he said, "why should your anger burn against your people, whom you brought out of Egypt with great power and a mighty hand? Why should the Egyptians say, 'It was with evil intent that he brought them out, to kill them in the mountains and to wipe them off the face of the earth'? Turn from your fierce anger; relent and do not bring disaster on your people. Remember your servants Abraham, Isaac and Israel, to whom you swore by your own self:

5WH PRAYER TECHNIQUE

'I will make your descendants as numerous as the stars in the sky and I will give your descendants all this land I promised them, and it will be their inheritance forever.'" Then the Lord relented and did not bring on his people the disaster he had threatened.
(Ex. 32:9-14NIV)

The passage above relates how Moses tactically used prayer to changed God's view and position regarding the situation his people were in, by engaging his glory and honor when he shifted God's attention from the sins of his people to what it would cost God if he eventually destroyed them.

First, Moses reminded God of what it cost to bring them out of Egypt (a great power and mighty hand), before speaking of what the Egyptians would say at the end of the day (it was with evil intent you brought them out, to destroy them in the mountain and wipe them from the face of the earth).

Remember, God told Moses in Exodus 9:16 and in 14:4 that the purpose for which he raised Pharaoh was to gain glory through him, so that his name (the Lord) will be proclaimed in all the earth. Destroying the Israelites in the desert would have aborted that plan and given the Egyptians an occasion to ridicule his great name.

The next thing Moses did was to remind God of how he swore by himself to Abraham, Isaac, and Jacob to increase their descendants and give them the land to inherit. This also engaged God's integrity and steadfastness, because killing them would imply that he is a covenant breaker. Just as everyone would do more to avoid pain than they would do to gain pleasure,

THE ORIGIN AND PURPOSE OF PRAYER

God had to change his mind from destroying the people, even though they deserved to die by reason of their sins, because of what it would cost him at the end of the day.

The cost of killing the people was way higher than the honor he would receive for destroying them (the Egyptians would ridicule him, his purpose would be aborted, his oath to the patriarchs would be undermined, his integrity and steadfastness questioned, and he would have been seen as evil and wicked God). This would have changed his nature, but God never changes. To prove this, he forgave his people and gave up his plans. The tactics and expertise Moses used to defend his people Israel before God that caused the Lord to spare them from destruction is the "How" method.

Another person who understands this technique and uses it to effectively produce positive results is father Abraham (I used this same story in my previous book to explain intercession strategy). The Scriptures below narrate how he tactically used the knowledge he had about the nature of God in the matter of justice, to defend a whole nation in prayer before him.

Since he knows God would not treat the righteous and the wicked the same, and knowing his wisdom in rendering justice, Abraham took advantage of it and wisely reminded God how unlawful it is for him to destroy the righteous with the wicked. He also pointed out to God, in an attempt to protect Sodom, that killing the righteous with the wicked would not be a noble act.

5WH PRAYER TECHNIQUE

For God to prove his steadfastness and integrity to Abraham, he agreed to abort the plan to destroy the land if he found in Sodom the number of righteous people father Abraham mentioned. Having identified this as a key factor he could use in his defense of Sodom, father Abraham took advantage of it and started bargaining for God to spare the land for the sake of few righteous people.

"Should I hide my plan from Abraham?" the Lord asked. "For Abraham will certainly become a great and mighty nation, and all the nations of the earth will be blessed through him. I have singled him out so that he will direct his sons and their families to keep the way of the Lord by doing what is right and just. Then I will do for Abraham all that I have promised." So the Lord told Abraham, "I have heard a great outcry from Sodom and Gomorrah, because their sin is so flagrant. I am going down to see if their actions are as wicked as I have heard. If not, I want to know." The other men turned and headed toward Sodom, but the Lord remained with Abraham. Abraham approached him and said, "Will you sweep away both the righteous and the wicked? Suppose you find fifty righteous people living there in the city—will you still sweep it away and not spare it for their sakes? Surely you wouldn't do such a thing, destroying the righteous along with the wicked. Why, you would be treating the righteous and the wicked exactly the same! Surely you wouldn't do that! Should not the Judge of all the earth do what is right?" And the Lord replied, "If I find fifty righteous people in Sodom, I will spare the entire city for their sake." (Gen.18:17-26NLT)

THE ORIGIN AND PURPOSE OF PRAYER

Abraham continued from fifty down to ten with strong arguments in favor of the land so it would not be destroyed, and God granted his request. Unfortunately, there were not ten righteous people in the whole land. Perhaps, if father Abraham had continued the negotiation until he got God to spare the entire land because of one righteous person, Sodom and Gomorrah would not have been destroyed.

However, he did what every true intercessor would do. He stood for them, stopped God from continuing his journey to the city, and gave him reasons to abort his plan to destroy the people. His tactical move, based on his knowledge and experience of who God is and how he works, would have delivered Sodom and Gomorrah from destruction had there been ten righteous people in the land.

Genesis 19:29, says God remembered Abraham and sent Lot out of the land when he destroyed it. Although Abraham's intercession couldn't save the whole land, it saved his nephew Lot as we observe in the Bible passage below.

Then Abraham spoke again. "Since I have begun, let me speak further to my Lord, even though I am but dust and ashes. Suppose there are only forty-five righteous people rather than fifty? Will you destroy the whole city for lack of five?" And the Lord said, "I will not destroy it if I find forty-five righteous people there." Then Abraham pressed his request further. "Suppose there are only forty?" And the Lord replied, "I will not destroy it for the sake of the forty." "Please don't be angry, my Lord," Abraham pleaded.

5WH PRAYER TECHNIQUE

"Let me speak—suppose only thirty righteous people are found?" And the Lord replied, "I will not destroy it if I find thirty." Then Abraham said, "Since I have dared to speak to the Lord, let me continue—suppose there are only twenty?" And the Lord replied, "Then I will not destroy it for the sake of the twenty." Finally, Abraham said, "Lord, please don't be angry with me if I speak one more time. Suppose only ten are found there?" And the Lord replied, "Then I will not destroy it for the sake of the ten." When the Lord had finished his conversation with Abraham, he went on his way, and Abraham returned to his tent.
(Gen.18:27-33NLT)

Whenever you read the Bible, try to decode the truth, concept, or principle that the verse, chapter, passage, or story establishes, and use it to analyze every related case you are facing. This will allow you to see things from God's point of view and understand his position in every situation. God will never act outside the parameters that the truths, concepts and principles in his written word (the Holy Bible) establish. Consequently, the measure of revelation knowledge and understanding of the written word of God that you have determines how well you can use this prayer method.

The "5WH Prayer Technique," which comprises the "What, Who and Whom, Why, When, Where, and How," is a practical and easy way to enhance your prayer. It teaches you the importance of the things you say in prayer, why you say them, when you say them, where you say the things, and how you say them.

THE ORIGIN AND PURPOSE OF PRAYER

It also highlights the important of knowing both who you are in Christ, and having a sound revelation knowledge about the God you serve.

The "5WH Prayer Technique" is a formula that works wonders! It gives you a clear and quick view about how prayer works, and the different factors that could either enhance your prayer life or work against you in prayer. The method allows you to understand the different factors that go into the prayer process, and the role each of them play to determine the kind of results we produce in prayer.

CHAPTER THREE

PERSONAL DEVOTION

In the words of my papa, the archbishop Duncan-Williams, "Prayer is the lifeline of the believer and is a vital key for walking in victory, however many Christians neglect to use this weapon of prayer. The Jews pray three times – a- day and Muslims pray five times – a – day, but many Christians only pray when they feel like it. How often do you pray?"

The number of times we are supposed to pray in a day as Christians is one of the questions people often ask whenever I teach on this subject. The other questions include: (1) whether we have a specific prayer timetable as Christians, according to scripture, (2) the specific time of the day we are supposed to pray, (3) whether or not some hours of the day are more convenient or important for prayer than others, (4) how long we should pray, (5) when we are supposed to stop praying about a particular thing, (6) what the minimum amount of time we are to spend in prayer is, according to Jesus' estimation, (7) how often we are to pray, according to the Bible.

THE ORIGIN AND PURPOSE OF PRAYER

The answers to the above questions are very simple, because it is clearly stated in the Scriptures. I am going to ask you to do a research and meditate on the questions. Normally, I give this assignment to those who take the class with me at the prayer school, and the results have always been incredible.

The exercise has helped a lot of people to go out of their way in search for the appropriate answers to the above questions from the Bible. It also helped some to enhance the effectiveness, and consistency of their prayer life when they started applying the truth they discovered from the written word of God.

All I can tell you is to read your Bible attentively, meditate on the different passages, do further research and ask the people around you what they think about the subject. Put the correct answers in the blank space below before you continue reading. This exercise may take you time, but it is worth doing. And by the time you finish it, you won't need anybody to tell you when to pray.

ANSWERS

1..
2..
3..
4..
5..
6..
7..
8..

PERSONAL DEVOTION

Personal devotion is taking time out to be alone with God. It allows you to have a quality quiet time with the Lord through Bible study, meditation, worship or prayer. When you spend time in God's presence, his glory rubs off on you. No one ever enters God's presence and leaves the same way. Something good always happen whenever you enter God's presence to worship and praise him. There is an anointing in God's presence that changes lives and situations.

The Bible declares in Ezekiel 46:9, that when the people come in through the north gate to worship the Lord during the religious festivals, they must leave by the south gate. And those who enter through the south gate must leave by the north gate. They must never leave by the same gate they came in, but must always use the opposite gate. You cannot spend quality time in God's presence and remain the same. Something special always happen, it could either be spiritual or physical in the life of those who spend time in the presence of God.

But when the people come in through the north gateway to worship the Lord during the religious festivals, they must leave by the south gateway. And those who entered through the south gateway must leave by the north gateway. They must never leave by the same gateway they came in, but must always use the opposite gateway. (Ezek. 46:9-10NLT)

Personal devotion enhances spiritual growth and maturity. It raises your spiritual antenna, makes you sensitive to spiritual things, draws you closer to God, and separates you from the world.

THE ORIGIN AND PURPOSE OF PRAYER

Make it a habit to find a convenient time in the course of the day to be alone with the Lord. When you make time for God, he enriches it and makes your life fruitful.

The portion of scriptures below relates how Moses left the camp to the top of Mount Sinai for an encounter with God. Having separated himself from everything, he tarried in the presence of the Lord forty days and night without eating bread or drinking water in order to receive the words of the covenant, which is the "Ten Commandments." Throughout the time Moses remained in God's presence, he spoke with the Lord but he didn't know that the glory of God rubbed off on him.

When he finally came down from Mount Sinai, he wasn't aware that his face was radiant because he had spoken with the Lord. By the time those he left behind in the camp saw the glory of God radiating from his face, they were afraid to come near him. He had to cover his face with a veil before the people could approach him. This is what happens when you spent quality time in God's presence.

Moses was there with the Lord forty days and forty nights without eating bread or drinking water. And he wrote on the tablets the words of the covenant — the Ten Commandments. When Moses came down from Mount Sinai with the two tablets of the Testimony in his hands, he was not aware that his face was radiant because he had spoken with the Lord. When Aaron and all the Israelites saw Moses, his face was radiant, and they were afraid to come near him. But Moses called to them; so Aaron and all the leaders of the community came back to him, and he spoke to them.

PERSONAL DEVOTION

Afterward all the Israelites came near him, and he gave them all the commands the Lord had given him on Mount Sinai. When Moses finished speaking to them, he put a veil over his face. But whenever he entered the Lord's presence to speak with him, he removed the veil until he came out. And when he came out and told the Israelites what he had been commanded.
(Ex. 34:28-34NIV)

But Jesus often withdrew to lonely places and prayed.
(Lk. 5:16NIV)

No matter how busy you are, try and make time to be alone with God. It will change your life for good and make you more effective in your field of activities. When you come into the presence of the Lord, he renews your strengths and empowers you to fulfil your assignment. To have a consistent quality time with the Lord, you have to set up a prayer closet.

As I explained in my other book, Understanding the Art of Prayer, under the heading "The Secret place of God," the prayer Closet can be defined as a place for personal encounter with the Lord. My papa the Archbishop Duncan-Williams calls it a place where divinity meets humanity. God's agenda for humanity is enforced in the place of prayer.

The power and authority to birth God's kingdom and superimpose his will over the kingdom of men, and the works of the wicked, is activated in the prayer closet. None is so powerful and influential on earth than the person who dwells in the prayer closet, and control things from a higher dimension. When you spend time in the presence of God, his glory and power rubs off on you.

HOW TO START PERSONAL QUIET TIME

Select a specific time: it is very important you chose a specific time that is convenient for you to be alone with God. Don't chose the time that coincide with other activities so you won't keep putting it off. If you keep postponing your quiet time with the Lord, you will end up losing the passion to ever do it.

Have a plan or agenda: to be more effective and consistent, plan your activities so you can maximize the little time you put aside. You could start with thanksgiving, praise or worship, Bible reading, meditation, and prayer. Whatever way you chose to do it, make sure you have a plan.

Chose a particular place: I suggest you find a convenient place, where you won't be distracted. Some use the restroom during lunch break as a place to encounter the Lord whenever they are free. It depends on the condition, rules and regulations that govern the place you work. Just make sure you chose a place and time that is convenient for you. If you want to do it at home, chose a place that is convenient for you.

Go to bed on time: don't go to bed late and expect to wake up early and be strong for prayer, if you are planning early Morning Prayer time with God. The Bible shows us how the Lord Jesus took Peter, James and John to a place called Gethsemane for a time of prayer. "My soul is overwhelmed with sorrow to the point of death. Stay here and keep watch with me," he said to them as he went a little farther to pray.

When he returned to his disciples, he found they sleeping. "Could you not keep watch with me for one hour?" He asked Peter.

PERSONAL DEVOTION

Then he noticed that though they were willing to do it, their body was weak. Therefore, he said "The spirit is willing, but the body is weak." (Matt.26:36-41). When the body is weak, the spirit can't do much. Go to bed on time, and wakeup early so you can have a quality time with God in the early hour of the day.

Once you wake up, get up immediately: once the time you fixed for the encounter comes and you awaken, please don't remain in bed. Not even for a second. Chances are you may fall asleep if you remain comfortably in that bed. If you wake up and feel very drowsy, find a way to break the pattern. Some people would wash their face in the restroom. Others would start walking around and singing immediately. Look for the one that work best for you and use it when the need arises.

Don't make it too long: I always encourage people to start with 15 or 20 minutes, and then increase the amount of time once you start getting used to it. When you start with one hour, there is high tendency you may be discouraged if you are not used to praying for a long time. More especially when you don't have much to pray about. To be on the safe side, make it as short as possible and gradually increase the amount of time, if you have to do so.

Be consistent and committed: consistency is very important as it relates to personal devotion. Because many things would come your way to stop you from having the quality time with the Lord. To prevent that from happening, commit yourself to it and make it a duty. I used the word duty because it is a responsibility. Until you begin to see it from this point of view, and make it a top priority, you may have difficulty committing yourself to it.

THE ORIGIN AND PURPOSE OF PRAYER

A number of times, I have met some people who started their personal quiet time with so much enthusiasm that they always look forward to the hour that they had set aside to be alone with God, and would not allow anything on earth to hinder them from having the sweet fellowship at first, until the day they finally realized that they have lost the zeal and time for the life changing encounter with God.

When I asked them about how it all happened, some would say it is the devil, others would give some funny excuses like having too many things to do, coming home late and tired, not having some free time etc. but when you look at it critically, you would notice the main reason is negligence. To avoid that, make it a priority, and commit yourself to it.

Choose the best posture that is appropriate for you: to be effective in prayer, you need to adopt the posture that work best for you. Some people kneel in prayer, others walk around, and few preferred to stand, while some few others either take a seat or lie on the floor. For me, I always prefer to stand when praying unless standing may not be appropriate at the place I am at. In that case, I either take a seat or kneel down to pray. Generally speaking, I feel more comfortable standing and walking around when praying than any other position. Tryout the different posture and choose the one that work best for you.

If you live with family members that share the same faith with you, share the vision with them and pray together if possible. Some in the house may want to pray but do not know how to go about it. Inviting such person can be a way to encourage, and motivate the individual to pray. Don't keep it to yourself alone. Share with others, and help them to enhance their prayer life.

PERSONAL DEVOTION

Respect time so you don't discourage the other person praying with you. This is very important when you are praying with other members of the family. You have to understand that everybody is not you, and they do not necessarily see things from your point of view. You may have reasons for intending to exceed the time you all agreed on, but it may not work well for everyone.

If you live with people who don't share your faith, please use wisdom when you are praying. Don't wake up at the middle of the night and start singing or praying loudly to disturb the other people from sleeping. Something happened at my house one day, when a friend visited and decided to pray at the early hour of the day beginning from 3 a.m. to about 5 a.m. His voice was so loud that my neighbors could not sleep.

The first thing they did in the morning was to report me to the landlord and insist he gives a quit notice. I had to explain things to him, and make new commitment before he could allow me to continue in the house. It is very important we use wisdom wherever we are at.

If you wake before time, and you are comfortable with praying, do it. When you set a time for prayer, you would want to wait till that very hour comes before you pray. However, God may wake you earlier to deal with certain things in the spirit. The Scriptures declares that as the heavens are higher than the earth, so are his ways higher than our ways (Is.55:9). Don't make the mistake of trying to force yourself to sleep, especially if the time is close. Just get up and pray.

Keep learning some basic prayer techniques that work and apply them during your prayers. Read about prayer, listen to sermons on the subject, and attend seminars or conferences that would enhance your prayer life.

HINTS FOR PERSONAL BIBLE STUDY

The measure of the revelation knowledge of the word of God that you have would determine the effectiveness and consistency of your prayer life. The simplest way to enhance your prayer life is to enrich yourself with the word of God and practice what you learn in prayer. I would like to share with you, a very simple method that I have used over the years for Bible studies. It has helped me a lot in different ways to achieve better results in the things of God. There are basically four methods that I use, depending on the goals I want to achieve.

First: Daily Bible Reading – the daily Bible reading plan has helped me tremendously, because it allows me to read through the entire books of the Bible every year. And since I have done that many times, it helps me to remember the different Bible stories and events. It keeps the passages fresh in my mind. There are different daily Bible reading plans available today, but I always use the one that allows me to finish the whole Bible (Old and New Testaments), in a year with morning and evening schedule.

Some focus on the New Testament in the morning, and the Old Testament in the evening, while others do it the other way round. Whatever way, is ok by me. The Old Testament introduces me to the New, while the New connects me to the Old and gives me more information about it. Whether I start my day with the New or Old Testament, I am always able to make the connections.

The only advice I can give you regarding this is that it works. But you are free to choose the one that work best for you. Find a well-planned and consistent way to read your Bible daily. It will greatly enrich the measure of the knowledge of God's word that you have.

PERSONAL DEVOTION

Second: Word or Topic Study Method – this is another good way to study the Bible. This method allows me to cover a subject or topic in its entirety by reading different verses of scriptures that talk about it. For example, since I started writing this book, I have looked up numerous Bible reference that talked about prayer. I am constantly in search for passages from Genesis to Revelation that talked about the subject to mediate and research. At times, I also look up other topics that are related to what I am dealing with right now.

There are several topics you can research or meditate. Examples includes faith, love, sin, relationship, sowing, giving, offense, forgiveness and so on. To do this successfully, you would need some Bible studies tools like Bible Concordance, Study Bible, Dictionaries, Commentaries, Greek and Hebrew lexicon. Depending on what you want to work on.

Third: Book Studies – I do this to gain insight to who wrote the books of the Bible, when it was written, where the author did the work, why he had to write it, and how it was written. The political, social-economic, spiritual, or moral state of the people at the time it was written.

This method reveals some important background information about the book that would help you to interpret the passage correctly. It allows you to understand some significant features, events, circumstances that shaped the world and the thought pattern of the writers at the time they wrote the book, so you can established the right connections between their world and the one we are living in so as to have a clear idea of the life and situations of people at the time.

THE ORIGIN AND PURPOSE OF PRAYER

With this method, you approach Bible texts and passages from the inside out. You won't just take things from the surface, but you dig from the root. Just like the Topic Study Method, you would need some tools like: Study Bible, Dictionaries, Commentaries, Greek and Hebrew lexicon etc.

Fourth: Bible Characters – this is very interesting because it allows you to explore the life of Bible characters to learn from their life experiences, such as their birthplace and conditions, growth, success, failure, strength, weakness, mistake and so on. You can learn about how they started life and where they ended it. How God works with the individual Bible character, and find the best way to apply whatever lessons you learn from them.

There are many great Bible character that you could follow closely by reading the different books of the Bible that talk about them. Father Abraham, Jacob, Isaac, Moses, Joshua, Samson, Gideon, Jephthah, Jabez, Ruth, Samuel, Saul, David, Solomon, Hezekiah, Jehoshaphat, Deborah, Isaiah, Elijah, Elisha, Ezekiel, Daniel, Elizabeth, Mary, the Lord Jesus and the Apostles, and so on.

Before I forget, I would like to say that though I basically use these four methods for personal Bible studies, I don't use them simultaneously. There is time for everything says the written word of God. I only employ the one that most serve the need I have at the time I'm studying. As earlier said, it all depends on the targets I have in mind. Chose the method that meets your need, depending on the goal you want to achieve.

CHAPTER FOUR

MORNING GLORY PRAYER

Morning glory prayer is a time reserve for personal devotion. It is all about rising early in the morning to have a personal encounter with the Lord in prayer. It begins with a time set aside in the morning to be alone with the Lord through Bible reading, meditation, worship or prayer. The Bible recounts how the Lord Jesus rose early in the morning to a solitary place for prayer and fellowship with the Father.

And rising very early in the morning, while it was still dark, he departed and went out to a desolate place, and there he prayed. (Mk.1:35ESV)

Yet the news about him spread all the more, so that crowds of people came to hear him and to be healed of their sicknesses. But Jesus often withdrew to lonely places and prayed.
(Lk. 5:15-16NIV)

The Lord Jesus maintained a consistent personal devotion with the Father, by rising early in the morning and late in the evening to fellowship with him.

THE ORIGIN AND PURPOSE OF PRAYER

To command your day and decide what happens each day, you must be an early riser. The one who rises early in the morning to pray always commands their day, and determines what happens in the course of the day. The Lord Jesus went to the mountains, deserts and other solitary places for a quiet time with the Father in prayer.

Have you commanded the morning since your days began and caused the dawn to know its place, So that [light] may get hold of the corners of the earth and shake the wickedness [of night] out of it? (Job 38:12-13AMP)

The passage above talks about commanding or giving order to the day. I like the way the *Holman Christian Standard Bible* puts it, "Have you ever in your life commanded the morning or assigned the dawn its place, so it may seize the edges of the earth and shake the wicked out of it?" You can order your day, and decide how your morning would be, by programming it through prayer. If not, God wouldn't have asked his servant Job whether he has ever commanded his morning and shown his dawn its place.

To do this, wake up early, lift up prayer and speak to the day, program every moment of the entire day and decide how you would want it to be. Command your feet to lead you to the place of divine appointment when you shall step out of your home in the morning, order your hands to attract and handle fortune, overturn every negative prediction and projection that the wicked already programmed in the stars, moon, sun, air or ground through enchantment, divination, sorcery, evil sacrifice, incantation, and so on. Block all demonic surprises and aggressions, and release the fire of the Holy Spirit to consume every evil seed the wicked sown that is waiting to manifest in the course of the day.

MORNING GLORY PRAYER

Finally, secure your life and properties; silence the voices of wickedness and superimpose the predetermine counsel of God on all that will take place during the day.

Luke 22:44-46 narrates how the Lord Jesus earnestly prayed until his sweat fell to the ground like drops of blood. When he finally rose from prayer and went back to his disciples, he found them asleep, exhausted from sorrow. He said to them, "Why are you sleeping? Get up and pray so that you will not fall into temptation."

In my opinion, I think for the Lord to ask his disciples to pray in order not to fall into temptation means the power to prevent evil or avoid temptation can be activated through prayer. Otherwise, he wouldn't have asked them to do it.

People who command their day, and order their steps in prayer by rising early in the morning, always escape the snare of the wicked in the course of the day. Make it a habit to rise early and program your day in prayer.

Hear what the Psalmist says in chapter 88:13, "But I cry to you Lord; in the morning my prayer comes before you." The man understands the importance of rising early in the morning to fellowship with the Lord. His prayer goes before God in the morning.

Give ear to my words, O Lord, consider my sighing. Listen to my cry for help, my King and my God, for to you I pray. In the morning, O Lord, you hear my voice; in the morning I lay my requests before you and wait in expectation.
(Ps.5:1-3NIV)

He makes his requests known to God in the morning, and waits patiently for God to come through for him in the day.

THE ORIGIN AND PURPOSE OF PRAYER

The principle of firstfruit, says the first governs the rest, and it sets a precedent for whatever follows. When you give God the very first hours of your day, he secures the rest of the day for you.

Morning glory prayer is one of the best and easiest ways to do that, because it allows you to set some time apart in the early hour of the day for personal encounter with the Lord, before you begin your daily activity. None has ever encounter God and remains the same.

When the Lord takes the first hour of your day, he takes care of the other hours for you. I encourage you to take time out every morning to be alone with the Lord through Bible studies, meditation, worship, and prayer.

I have also sent to you all My servants the prophets, rising up early and sending them, saying, 'Turn now everyone from his evil way, amend your doings, and do not go after other gods to serve them; then you will dwell in the land which I have given you and your fathers.' But you have not inclined your ear, nor obeyed Me.
(Jer. 35:15 NKJV)

This portion of scripture reveals that God is an early riser. It says he gets up early to send his servants the prophets. People who get up early to fellowship with the Lord always encounter his glorious presence.

The Psalmist says in 119:147, "I rise before dawn and cry for help; I have put my hope in your word." King David and other great men and women of old had personal quality time with the Lord, and they also maintained a personal devotion through prayer, sacrifice, fellowship and dedication. They all cultivated the habit of rising early in the morning to meet with God for instruction, direction, empowerment, communion etc. In the end, they all lived a life of impact, changed their world, and left positive legacies for the generation that came after them.

CHAPTER FIVE

FAMILY ALTAR

A family altar is a place and time set aside for Bible study, meditation, fellowship, worship, and prayer. It is a place where members of the family gather for an encounter with the Lord. A family that prays together stays together says, one of my pastor friends. The easiest way and place to teach and establish Biblical principles, and core values that shape and guide members of the family, is at the altar of prayer.

When God visited the Israelites in Egypt, and delivered them from the hand of the Egyptians, they were all born, raised, educated and trained according to the pattern, belief system, mentality, practices, culture, and traditions of Egypt, which was totally different from God's ways, standard and pattern of doing things. Second, the land of Canaan he promised to their fathers for an inheritance was occupied by a different people with culture, belief system, mentality, tradition, mode of worship, characters, and habits that is also different from what he intend for his people.

THE ORIGIN AND PURPOSE OF PRAYER

Having redeemed them from Egypt, God had to find a neutral ground, where he could introduce his ways, principles, concepts, standard, practices, and the central truth about himself to his people in order to create a paradigm shift in their mind by deprogramming all that they learned in Egypt, and reprogramming it with the law he gave to Moses as a way of protecting them against what the people in the land of Canaan prepared to offer them.

The systems both in Egypt and Canaan land allow the people to believe in the worship of multiple gods, and indulge in certain practices that God disallows. To correct the error and pattern of Egypt, he revealed his laws to Moses, laid down principles, precepts, and pattern that is totally different from that of Egypt, which the people were used to. He also built the Tabernacle and introduced a new way of worship with all its utensils and requirements. The Lord used this to establish new parameters, lines, and boundaries as to what is allowed or unlawful in accordance with his laws and principles.

God started a whole new process of transformation to deliver his people from the grips of Egypt, and also to protect them against the snare of Canaan land. He took them through different kinds of things to build new experiences that would shape their belief systems with new references. Actions produce experiences, which establish references that build and strengthen beliefs.

When you go through something, it becomes an experience that you could sometime refer to along the line, and when such experience reoccurs, it becomes a reference point and a lens through which you examine and view other similar issues.

FAMILY ALTAR

For example, when the Lord told them human does not live by bread alone as they have always done in Egypt, but by the word that proceeds from his mouth, he proves it by allowing them to hunger, before giving them manna to eat. He gave them strict instruction regarding the manna to obey before they could have it for food (Deut.8:3).

For this process of reformation and transformation to be successful, God didn't initiate it in Egypt neither did he wait for them to arrive Canaan land before introducing it. Both Egypt and Canaan are types of the World that surround us today, while the camp in the wilderness represents our respective homes and families. To effect his purpose in their lives, God came and dwelled amongst them in the camp. And gave them the following instruction, through the mouth of his servant Moses.

And you must love the Lord your God with all your heart, all your soul, and all your strength. And you must commit yourselves wholeheartedly to these commands that I am giving you today. Repeat them again and again to your children. Talk about them when you are at home and when you are on the road, when you are going to bed and when you are getting up. Tie them to your hands and wear them on your forehead as reminders. Write them on the doorposts of your house and on your gates.
(Deut. 6:5-9 NLT)

The Lord commanded the Israelite in the above scripture to teach their children all the things they learned about him, including his laws and principles, when they are in the house, on the road, when going to bed, and when getting up in the morning. So that the younger generation can learn about his works and ways, laws and principles, patterns, culture and practices.

THE ORIGIN AND PURPOSE OF PRAYER

When this becomes part of them, it will give them a sense of who they really are, why they exist, and what they stand for. The laws and principles of God establish values, lines and boundaries that allow us to stay on track wherever we found ourselves.

The same way God chose the camp, where all members of the family of the Israelites met and discus about his works, to introduce his laws and principles, the family altar is the most suitable place for establishing moral values and principles that shape the life and destinies of the members of the family. An easy way to do this is to choose a time that is convenient for the members of the family to gather for a quality time in the presence of God, through Bible study, meditation, worship and prayer.

A family altar establishes the presence and authority of God in a home. When you give God the preeminence in your home by placing him at the center of everything in your house, through Bible study, meditation, fellowship, worship, and prayer, he establishes his reign, presence and authority in your family.

HOW TO INITIATE FAMILY ALTAR

If members of the family share your faith, explain the importance of praying together as a family to them, and start doing it. I have seen some cases were people live with members of their family that do not attend the same church with them, but shares the same faith. At the same time, I have also seen instances were members of the same family living in the same house, shares different faith and religion. If your case is the first, explain things to others, invite them and see whether it is possible to pray with them.

FAMILY ALTAR

Many would rather hide in their room and pray alone, than find a way to make the other people in their house join them in prayer. Remember you are the light of the world according to the written word of God. No one lights a lamp and puts it under a bowl. Instead, a lamp is placed on a stand, where it gives light to everyone in the house. Let your light shine!

You are the light of the world—like a city on a hilltop that cannot be hidden. No one lights a lamp and then puts it under a basket. Instead, a lamp is placed on a stand, where it gives light to everyone in the house. In the same way, let your good deeds shine out for all to see, so that everyone will praise your heavenly Father.
(Matt.5:14-16NLT)

Choose a time that is convenient for members of the family to gather. The fact you are free by 6 or 7, whether morning or evening, does not necessarily mean everybody is free at that time. You need to think and plan with the other person in mind. The hour that works for you may not be convenient for them. So chose one that is most convenient for all, be it in the evening before bedtime or early in the morning before leaving home.

Make sure you keep it simple, in order not to discourage others. The family altar is not the place for preaching Sunday morning sermons. Do all you can to make it very simple, fun and flexible so that everybody can participate regardless of their age. Find a way to make the subject for discussion relevant to everyone, and do not make it too long, start with 15 or 20 minutes.

THE ORIGIN AND PURPOSE OF PRAYER

Plan and prepare all the materials or instrument that you may use during the meeting for Bible Studies, praise and worship, prayer etc. It distracts when members of the family start moving around in search for the materials they want to use, when the meeting has already started. It is better to ensure everyone has the things they need before you start.

Avoid monotony; and get a new way to do the old thing. When it is too old, people lose interest, and if it is too new, they may be unable to connect. To make it interesting, always find a new and better way to do the old thing. Encourage everyone to participate in whatever best way they can, and encourage creativity as a way of improving the quality of the service. Make it interesting for all, regardless of their age group, so the kids would always find reasons to come.

Do not criticize or judge anyone no matter what they say or how they say it. Encourage open communication, promote love, forgiveness, honesty, and sharing. Make it a platform where members of the family could be free to say what is in their mind, and share their point of view about any issue that comes up as subject for discussion. Make sure everyone says something. There should be no spectator. Be consistent and committed.

IMPORTANCE OF FAMILY ALTAR

1. A family that prays together stays together – it unites the family members
2. It establishes God's sovereignty and authority in the family
3. It promotes oneness, love, and unity in the family
4. It enhances openness, and forgiveness among family members

FAMILY ALTAR

5. It enhances spiritual growth and maturity through Bible study and meditation
6. It establishes moral values, and principles that shape the life of family members
7. It attracts God's presence, blessings, and glory
8. It fends off the enemies, and keeps them out of the family
9. It establishes parameters, lines, and boundaries that keep family members on track
10. It is a good ground for sharing and receiving
11. It strengthens brotherly love, and parents and children relationship
12. It allows members of the family to know what they stand for and why they exist

There is no better place to instill your moral values, faith, belief, principles, and way of life in the members of your family than on the family altar.

I have a friend who taught his children the power of prayer, by using situations and events in his house to strengthen the faith and believe of his family members. He made the children to believe that God has the final say, and when he approves of anything, no one can resist it.

He shared with me one day of how his boss promoted him, and the whole thing was supposed to take effect from the following month. When he got home, he shared it with his wife. Both of them used the situation to strengthen the faith of their children, by calling them at the hour of prayer and sharing with them how a lot of loyal and very committed people at his place of work labor so hard, but get no promotion because of injustice.

THE ORIGIN AND PURPOSE OF PRAYER

While those who often get the promotion sometimes don't deserve it.

That very day, he told them he felt it was time for him to be promoted at his work place because of the contribution he has made to the company, but something was blocking it. If they could all petition heaven for the release of the promotion, things will change for good in the family. They all prayed earnestly and kept at it for some weeks until the day, when he finally came home with the promotion letter.

The first thing his children said is, "Daddy, prayer works! We prayed for God to promote you and he did it." This experience made the children to believe that God answers prayer, and that you can get whatever you want from him through prayer.

Starting from that moment, whenever there is a situation, the first course of action his children always suggest is prayer. And having done it several times with many positive results, nothing on earth can make his children doubt the miracle working power of prayer and God's ability to do the impossible.

Today, those children have many experiences and references to back up their belief that they get offended whenever someone tries to speak against prayer and God's ability to work miracles.

There are many ways to do this, God himself knows our needs, and he creates the desire in us to make us petition him for it, before giving the thing to us. This whole process of having a need, desiring it, praying earnestly about the thing, and receiving it in a miraculous way, establishes a pattern in our mind that shapes our world.

CHAPTER SIX

PRAYER RETREAT

This is a time set aside for the sole purpose of seeking the Lord. It is all about withdrawing from the pressures and demand of our daily activities and duties for a quiet time with God. It is very important to withdraw from your normal routine to worship God, pray, read the Bible and meditate.

We are living in a time when almost everything is done at a very high speed. Time is precious, demands are high, works are increasing, innovation is at its peak, things are changing so fast that everybody is becoming more and more busy, doing all they can to catch up with the speed at which the world is moving in order to meet up with the pressure and demand of the day.

Due to the nature of the work some people do, they are caught up in activities and routines that take almost everything from them at the end of the day. They are either exhausted, stressed, confused, worried, nervous, uneasy, vexed, depressed, sick or totally emptied.

THE ORIGIN AND PURPOSE OF PRAYER

Some are even cutoff from the real world, living in the shadow, and losing connection with the most important things around them (including God, themselves and the wonderful people that surround them).

It is so important that you withdraw from your normal routine, to a different place or location for a time of refreshing in the presence of God, to separate and empty your mind from anxiety by communing with the Lord through worship, praise, prayer, or Bible meditation.

The Bible declares in Matthew 11:28, "Come to me all you who are weary and burdened, and I will give you rest." The Lord Jesus also promised in John 6:37, "All that the Father gives me will come to me, and whoever comes to me I will never cast out." When you take time out from your busy schedule to be alone with God on a prayer retreat, he will meet you at the very point of your needs, and your life will never again be the same.

Exodus 19:17-20 relates how Moses led the people of Israel from the camp to the foot of the mountain for an encounter with the Lord. It says Mount Sinai was covered with smoke because the Lord had descended on it in the form of fire, which caused the whole mountain to shake violently. When the sound of the trumpet increased, Moses spoke, and God answered him in thunder.

The Israelites had this incredible experience because they withdrew from their normal activities in the camp, went to the wilderness and stood at the foot of the mountain to meet with God.

PRAYER RETREAT

And since we serve a faithful God, scriptures declares that God also came down from heaven to the mountain top, where his people had come to worship him. When you retreat from work to be alone with God, he also comes to you for a life changing encounter and experience.

Then Moses brought the people out of the camp to meet God, and they took their stand at the foot of the mountain. Now Mount Sinai was wrapped in smoke because the Lord had descended on it in fire. The smoke of it went up like the smoke of a kiln, and the whole mountain trembled greatly. And as the sound of the trumpet grew louder and louder, Moses spoke, and God answered him in thunder. The Lord came down on Mount Sinai, to the top of the mountain. And the Lord called Moses to the top of the mountain, and Moses went up. (Ex.19:17-20ESV)

A closer look at the passage below teaches us the importance God places on retreat. It reveals how God set the bush ablaze in order to get Moses' attention, because he was too busy about tending the flock of his father-in-law.

Moses was a vessel God choose to liberate his people from Egypt and lead them to Canaan, a land he promised to father Abraham. For some reasons, Moses ended up in Median, where he lived with Jethro, who gave him his daughter Zipporah in marriage and put him in charge of his flock to feed and keep it.

Now Moses was tending the flock of Jethro his father-in-law, the priest of Midian, and he led the flock to the far side of the desert and came to Horeb, the mountain of God. There the angel of the Lord appeared to him in flames of fire from within a bush. Moses saw that though the bush was on fire it did not burn up.

THE ORIGIN AND PURPOSE OF PRAYER

So Moses thought, "I will go over and see this strange sight — why the bush does not burn up." When the Lord saw that he had gone over to look, God called to him from within the bush, "Moses! Moses!" And Moses said, "Here I am." "Do not come any closer," God said. "Take off your sandals, for the place where you are standing is holy ground." Then he said, "I am the God of your father, the God of Abraham, the God of Isaac and the God of Jacob." At this, Moses hid his face, because he was afraid to look at God. The Lord said, "I have indeed seen the misery of my people in Egypt. I have heard them crying out because of their slave drivers, and I am concerned about their suffering. So I have come down to rescue them from the hand of the Egyptians and to bring them up out of that land into a good and spacious land, a land flowing with milk and honey — the home of the Canaanites, Hittites, Amorites, Perizzites, Hivites and Jebusites. And now the cry of the Israelites has reached me, and I have seen the way the Egyptians are oppressing them. So now, go. I am sending you to Pharaoh to bring my people the Israelites out of Egypt."
(Ex 3:1-10 NIV)

Moses became so busy in his new home, feeding the flock of Jethro his father-in-law, the priest of Median that the Lord had to interrupt his daily routine by setting the bush on fire without actually burning the trees, in order to get his attention, and then unfold his plan for the Israelites to him.

The passage says the angel of the Lord appeared to him in a flame of fire from the middle of the bush. When Moses saw that though the bush was on fire it did not burn up, he said to himself, "I will go over and see why the bush is not burned." Verse 4 declares that when the Lord saw that Moses turned to take a closer look at the sight, he spoke to him from within the bush.

PRAYER RETREAT

We notice here that even though God had a special mission for Moses, he could not talk to him about it because Moses was too busy about his activities. He needed to separate from all distractions that clouded his mind and eyes from seeing.

Another good Bible passage that highlights the importance of withdrawing from our busy schedule to be alone with the Lord is 1Kings19:10-13. It talks about how the great prophet Elijah escaped the evil plot of Jezebel the wife of King Ahab to destroy him. Having travelled forty days and night from the desert of Beersheba in Judah, to Mount Sinai, he went into a cave and spent the night.

When God met him there, he asked, "What are you doing here Elijah?" he replied, "I have been very zealous for the Lord God Almighty. The Israelites have rejected your covenant, broken down your altars, and put your prophets to death with the sword. I am the only one left, and now they are trying to kill me too." At this, God instructed him to go out and stand on the mountain, while he passes by.

First, a powerful wind tore the mountains apart and shattered the rocks before the Lord, but God was not in the wind. Second, after the wind, there was an earthquake, but the Lord was not in the earthquake. Third, after the earthquake, a fire came, but the Lord was not in the fire either. Lastly, when the fire ended, there was a sound of a gentle whisper. As soon as Elijah heard it, he wrapped his face in his mantle, went out and stood at the entrance of the cave.

THE ORIGIN AND PURPOSE OF PRAYER

Everyone would have expected the prophet Elijah to encounter God when the earthquake, wind and fire tore the mountains apart and devastated everything on the way, but the Scripture clearly states that the still small voice (whisper), came at the time when the earthquake, fire, noise and distractions ended.

It stands to reason that we need to separate from certain things that take our time, attention, and occupy our mind to be alone with God in order to hear clearly from him. Otherwise, we may not hear from God or experience him the way he desires because too many voices are speaking into our ears. God is not a talkative!

Elijah replied, "I have zealously served the Lord God Almighty. But the people of Israel have broken their covenant with you, torn down your altars, and killed every one of your prophets. I am the only one left, and now they are trying to kill me, too." "Go out and stand before me on the mountain," the Lord told him. And as Elijah stood there, the Lord passed by, and a mighty windstorm hit the mountain. It was such a terrible blast that the rocks were torn loose, but the Lord was not in the wind. After the wind there was an earthquake, but the Lord was not in the earthquake. And after the earthquake there was a fire, but the Lord was not in the fire. And after the fire there was the sound of a gentle whisper. When Elijah heard it, he wrapped his face in his cloak and went out and stood at the entrance of the cave. And a voice said, "What are you doing here, Elijah?"
(1 Ki.19:10-13 NLT)

The noise, worries, pressure of the day can hinder us from hearing from the Lord.

PRAYER RETREAT

In the midst of the great and strong wind, earthquake and fire, the prophet Elijah could not hear God's voice until there was total silence.

Prayer retreat is a time of separation from normal routine, and activities to be alone with the Lord for Bible study, meditation, worship, and prayer. The passage below shows what the Lord Jesus did when his apostles returned and reported what they had done and taught. He said to them, "Come with me by yourself to a quiet place and get some rest." The reason he said this is because so many people were coming and going that they did not have a chance to eat. They were very busy.

The apostles gathered around Jesus and reported to him all they had done and taught. Then, because so many people were coming and going that they did not even have a chance to eat, he said to them, "Come with me by yourselves to a quiet place and get some rest." So they went away by themselves in a boat to a solitary place.
(Mk. 6:30-32 NIV)

If the lord Jesus could ask his disciples to withdraw from their activities to a quiet place in order to rest, because so many people came in and went out that they did not find time to even eat, it means that you too have to withdraw from your busy schedule to refresh yourself in the presence of God. Please take some days off work. The truth is that, your company, business, world etc. will not end in your absence. Go to God for new ideas, direction, strength, empowerment etc.

HOW TO PLAN PRAYER RETREAT

PURPOSE – the first thing you have to settle in your mind before embarking on a prayer retreat is the primary object. You must be able to decide why you need to withdraw from the pressure and demand of the day to be alone with God, through Bible meditation, worship, praise, and prayer. When the purpose of a thing is not known, abuse is inevitable. Similarly, unless the purpose for the retreat is well defined and established, it may not profit you much.

TIME AND DATE – another important thing you have to settle before leaving home to wherever you plan to have the retreat, is the time and date. You have to be clear about when to start and finish. Decide on the time and date before you make the move.

LOCATION – the place you chose for the retreat is very important. Considering the goal of the retreat, which is to separate from the things that take your time, attention and occupy your mind. The best thing to do will be to make sure you move away from the habitual location, and cut every link between you and your daily routine so you can stay focus, and concentrate while in God's presence.

PLAN – make sure you plan your activities, based on the main reason you decide to withdraw from your activities to seek God's face. Having an agenda or plan of spiritual activities that you will do throughout the time you are spending in God's presence, will help you to stay focused, active and refreshed.

PRAYER RETREAT

Some examples of good activities you could do include: worship, praises, prayer, Bible reading and meditation, reading inspirational books and listening to messages that are related to the goal you set for the retreat.

LEAVE EVERY DEVICE THAT COULD DISTRACT YOU BEHIND. For example, computer, smartphones or other electronics devices that the enemy could easily use to interrupt and steal the quality time you planned to be alone with God. Disconnect yourself from your world, and empty your mind in order to receive from the Lord. When you are distracted, you cannot hear clearly from God.

However, if the main purpose for the retreat is to receive inspiration for writing, brainstorming, problem solving, you may want to go with some tools, and materials that would facilitate your work.

IMPORTANT QUESTIONS

1. Must we necessarily fast on a retreat?
2. Can we plan a retreat without involving fasting?
3. What is the minimum time for prayer according to Jesus?
4. How long should we pray?

ANSWERS

1. You can plan a retreat without fasting depending on your intention

THE ORIGIN AND PURPOSE OF PRAYER

2. One hour is the minimum time for prayer according to Jesus' estimation (Matt.26:40)

3. Pray without ceasing

Then he returned to his disciples and found them sleeping. "Could you men not keep watch with me for one hour?" he asked Peter. "Watch and pray so that you will not fall into temptation. The spirit is willing, but the body is weak."
(Matt 26:40-41NIV)

Then Jesus told his disciples a parable to show them that they should always pray and not give up.
(Lk.18:1NIV)

Pray without ceasing. (1Thes. 5:17ESV)

CHAPTER SEVEN

PREVAILING POWER OF PRAYER

There is a power that resides in prayer by virtue of its nature, which can be triggered and employed as weapon of warfare or intercession. It is called the prevailing power of prayer. When activated, it produces the miraculous, changes lives and situations, does the impossible, and moves the mighty hand that controls all things. There is no limit to the effect of this power of prayer, be it spiritual or physical because it connects God's ability to do things with the right of humans to act on earth to make the impossible happen at any time.

You can be a prophet, a teacher, a pastor, an apostle, an evangelist, but without a prayer life, you will eventually dry up, wither and disappear from the face of the Earth.

- Archbishop Nicholas Duncan-Williams

Acts 12:1-17 describes what happened in the days of the early apostles, when the power that resides on prayer by virtue of its nature was triggered by the church. It says King Herod Agrippa started persecuting some believers in the church, and he had the apostle James killed with the sword.

THE ORIGIN AND PURPOSE OF PRAYER

When the king saw how much it pleased the Jewish people, he also arrested Peter, who was considered as one of the pillars in the church, puts him in jail and placed him under the guard of four squads of soldiers each, with the intention of bringing him out for public trial after the Passover.

While Peter was in prison, the church came together and prayed earnestly for God to deliver him from the plot of Herod and the Jewish people. Don't forget that when the king rose against the apostle James, the church didn't do anything and he died.

But when the same king arrested Peter so he could destroy him the same way he did to James, the church stood their ground in prayer and triggered the prevailing power of prayer, which connected God's ability to do things with the right of man to act on earth, and overturned the wicked plot and prediction of Herod and the Jewish people against Peter. Had the church done the same for James when King Herod got hold of him, the prevailing power of prayer would have rescued him out of the king's hand and delivered him from death.

It was about this time that King Herod arrested some who belonged to the church, intending to persecute them. He had James, the brother of John, put to death with the sword. When he saw that this pleased the Jews, he proceeded to seize Peter also. This happened during the Feast of Unleavened Bread. After arresting him, he put him in prison, handing him over to be guarded by four squads of four soldiers each. Herod intended to bring him out for public trial after the Passover. So Peter was kept in prison, but the church was earnestly praying to God for him.
(Acts 12:1-5 NIV)

PREVAILING POWER OF PRAYER

By reason of the prayer of the church for Peter, the Lord deployed an angel the night before the day Herod had planned to bring him to trial and execute him.

Peter was sleeping between two soldiers, bound with two chains, while other soldiers stood guard at the prison gate. Suddenly, the angel appeared in the cell, struck Peter on the side to awaken him. "Quick, get up!" He said to him, and the chains in Peter's wrists fell off. Then the angel asked him to dress up, and led him out of the cell through the first and second guard posts until they came to the iron gate that leads to the city, which opened for them by itself. They passed through and walked down the street before the angel suddenly disappeared.

The night before Herod was to bring him to trial, Peter was sleeping between two soldiers, bound with two chains, and sentries stood guard at the entrance. Suddenly an angel of the Lord appeared and a light shone in the cell. He struck Peter on the side and woke him up. "Quick, get up!" he said, and the chains fell off Peter's wrists. Then the angel said to him, "Put on your clothes and sandals." And Peter did so. "Wrap your cloak around you and follow me," the angel told him. Peter followed him out of the prison, but he had no idea that what the angel was doing was really happening; he thought he was seeing a vision. They passed the first and second guards and came to the iron gate leading to the city. It opened for them by itself, and they went through it. When they had walked the length of one street, suddenly the angel left him. Then Peter came to himself and said, "Now I know without a doubt that the Lord sent his angel and rescued me from Herod's clutches and from everything the Jewish people were anticipating."

THE ORIGIN AND PURPOSE OF PRAYER

When this had dawned on him, he went to the house of Mary the mother of John, also called Mark, where many people had gathered and were praying. Peter knocked at the outer entrance, and a servant girl named Rhoda came to answer the door. When she recognized Peter's voice, she was so overjoyed she ran back without opening it and exclaimed, "Peter is at the door!" "You're out of your mind," they told her. When she kept insisting that it was so, they said, "It must be his angel." But Peter kept on knocking, and when they opened the door and saw him, they were astonished. Peter motioned with his hand for them to be quiet and described how the Lord had brought him out of prison. "Tell James and the brothers about this," he said, and then he left for another place.
(Acts12:6-17NIV)

When Peter finally arrived at the place where the church gathered to pray for him, he knocked the door, but the one who was supposed to open it didn't because she was astonished that Peter had escaped the mouth of the lion alive. Some of them even thought it was Peter's angel that visited them until he described how God brought him out of the prison. None ever thought Peter would survive the plot of Herod. However, he did because of the prevailing power of prayer that the church activated on his behalf, which made the impossible to happen for him.

The power that thwarted Herod's wicked agenda, overturned the Jewish evil prediction against Peter, gave the church the upper hand over their enemies, caused a great commotion among the soldiers over what has become of Peter, made those who sought to kill him (Peter) to die in his place,

PREVAILING POWER OF PRAYER

led to the death of king Herod Agrippa, and caused God's word to spread and flourish abundantly in the land, is what I call the *prevailing power of prayer.*

Another good example of how this prevailing power of power works is an account recorded in Luke22:28-30. The passage reveals how the Lord Jesus commended his disciples for the sacrifices they made to stay with him throughout his moment of trials and pains. It is not everyone who started with him that continues till the end as we observed in John6:60-66. Some of his disciples turned away and deserted him when he started teaching them hard things about the kingdom of heaven. However, the twelve apostles stood with him.

While he was about paying the ultimate price for the redemption of human souls from sin and death, he started revealing his plan to grant his disciples the right to eat and drink at his table, and sit on thrones judging the twelve tribes of Israel in the kingdom that his Father assigned to him.

At that moment, he looked at Peter, and said, "Simon, Simon, Satan has asked to sift you as wheat. But I have prayed for, Simon, that your faith may not fail. And when you have turned back, strengthen your brothers."

If I may ask, where was the devil when they all abandoned their activities and made all the sacrifices to follow Jesus? He didn't show his ugly face until the time the disciples are supposed to be honored for their services and sacrifices.

THE ORIGIN AND PURPOSE OF PRAYER

He waited for them to finish paying the price, before attempting to attack and hinder them from enjoying the fruits of their labor, investments and sacrifices.

I like how the Lord Jesus took both an aggressive and defensive move in prayer to fend Satan off, block the aggression, overturn his demand, and secure his disciples. This is what I call *spiritual warfare and intercession strategy* (for more information on this, please go to my other book, *Strategic Prayer*).

This same power that the Lord Jesus used to safeguard his disciples against satanic onslaught, and that gave them superiority of means over the agenda of their enemies, is the prevailing power of prayer. It works both as a defensive, and offensive weapon for those who know how to trigger and use it, whether in warfare or intercession. It produces the miraculous, and changes things. It causes you to prevail, overcome, conquer, defeat, win or succeed in prayer when it is well activated and employed.

CHAPTER EIGHT

HOLY CRY

There are several reasons why people cry these days. However, the most common is when negative things happen or when things don't go the way they expect. Beginning with the issue of what to eat, to how to eat, then to when, and where to eat. Some cry about their marriages, relationships, businesses, finances, children, health, projects and so on. Because they see it as the normal thing to do when things fall apart to ease their pains and attract the sympathy of others. Hence, when the storm of life is raging, and things seem to be out of control, they would resort to crying and weeping.

Merriam-Webster Dictionary, include in its definition of cry, the following, "To produce tears from your eyes often while making loud sounds because of pain, sorrow, or other emotions. To shout or say something loudly." *Cambridge Advanced Learner's Dictionary* – 3rd edition, also defines it as, "To produce tears as the result of a strong emoion, such as unhappiness or pain."

THE ORIGIN AND PURPOSE OF PRAYER

Problem is part of life, and there is none on earth without an issue. And as our faces varies from that of other people, so are our needs, challenges and the things that cause us pains. We are all going through something at different levels and areas of our lives. What seems to be a problem for one person, may not be for another. The truth is that we all have an issue, and we cry about something, whether in the open or in secret.

Nevertheless, we have to understand that though everyone cries about something, all cries are not the same. There is a cry that changes things. It is a cry like no other cry, because it commands the attention of both heaven and earth. It changes lives and situations. It moves the mighty hand that controls all things. It is the only cry that connects God's ability to do things with the right of man to act in order to produce the miraculous and effect changes on earth.

This cry that provokes the miraculous, works wonders, causes the heavens, and the earth to act, moves the mighty hand of God, changes lives and situations, is called the "Holy Cry." It is a cry like no other, and it has the power to change destinies, bring the dead to life, heal the sick, cause the barren womb to conceive, make the poor rich, make the weak strong, turn the victim to victor, free the captives, open the heaven's door and cause the impossible to happen.

There are many instances in the Bible when renowned men and women of old raised their voices in holy cry to God, because of the situations that they were in at the time, and moved his hand to action in their favor.

HOLY CRY

A very good example is a passage in Exodus 2:23-25, that describes how the Israelites groaned because of their slavery, and cried out to God for help. The passage tells us that their cry for help went up to God, and he (the Lord) heard their groans, and remembered his covenant with Abraham, Isaac, and Jacob.

For this reason, the Lord moved to Median in search for Moses, who was the vessel he chose to liberate his people from bondage, bring them out of Egypt and lead them to the promise land. Had it not been for their groaning and cry for help that went up to God, the Lord wouldn't have gone out of his way to free them from bondage. Their holy cry provokes their deliverance, and catapulted them into their prophetic destiny.

Years passed, and the king of Egypt died. But the Israelites continued to groan under their burden of slavery. They cried out for help, and their cry rose up to God. God heard their groaning, and he remembered his covenant promise to Abraham, Isaac, and Jacob. He looked down on the people of Israel and knew it was time to act. (Ex.2:23-25)

Another good example is the story of the blind man called Bartimeus, who cried out to the Lord Jesus for help. The passage says as the Lord was leaving Jericho with his disciples, a large crowd followed him. It happened that when the blind man heard that it was Jesus of Nazareth passing by, he started crying out to him, "Jesus, Son of David, have mercy on me."

Many rebuked him and told him to be quiet, but he cried out all the more for mercy until his cry got Jesus attention. The Lord stopped and asked the people to call him.

THE ORIGIN AND PURPOSE OF PRAYER

On his arrival, Jesus asked him, "What do you want me to do for you?" the blind man answered, "Rabbi, I want to see." Immediately, the man received his sight and followed Jesus on the way.

Had he not cried out to the Lord Jesus about his situation, he would not have been healed. His cry to the Lord for mercy, turned his situation around and made his life better than it was before. This is one of the things that happen when people raise their voices in holy cry to the God of heaven and earth, for mercy. The result is that it changes their lives and situations.

Then they came to Jericho. As Jesus and his disciples, together with a large crowd, were leaving the city, a blind man, Bartimaeus (that is, the Son of Timaeus), was sitting by the roadside begging. When he heard that it was Jesus of Nazareth, he began to shout, "Jesus, Son of David, have mercy on me!" Many rebuked him and told him to be quiet, but he shouted all the more, "Son of David, have mercy on me!" Jesus stopped and said, "Call him." So they called to the blind man, "Cheer up! On your feet! He's calling you." Throwing his cloak aside, he jumped to his feet and came to Jesus. "What do you want me to do for you?" Jesus asked him. The blind man said, "Rabbi, I want to see." "Go," said Jesus, "your faith has healed you." Immediately he received his sight and followed Jesus along the road.
(Mk.10:46-52NIV)

Hebrews5:7-10 informs us that while the Lord Jesus was here on earth, he offered up prayers and petitions, with a loud cry and tears to the one who could save him from death, and he was heard because of his reverence for God.

HOLY CRY

Isn't it amazing to know that the Lord Jesus himself also raised a holy cry to the Father for divine intervention because of the situation he was in at the time?

The holy cry commands heaven's attention and moves the hand of God. This is why I call it a cry like no other, because of its ability to change life and situation. It is the only cry that brings permanent solution to the issues of life.

Some cry to feel better, others cry to get people's attention, and sympathy, while a few others cry to move the heavens and the earth to action. Those who engage in holy cries, are the ones that cause the heavens and earth to act.

In the days of his flesh, Jesus offered up prayers and supplications, with loud cries and tears, to him who was able to save him from death, and he was heard because of his reverence. Although he was a son, he learned obedience through what he suffered. And being made perfect, he became the source of eternal salvation to all who obey him, being designated by God a high priest after the order of Melchizedek.
(Heb. 5:7-10ESV)

From noon until three in the afternoon darkness came over the whole land. At about three in the afternoon Jesus cried out with a loud voice, "Elí, Elí, lemá sabachtháni?" that is, "My God, My God, why have You forsaken Me?" When some of those standing there heard this, they said, "He's calling for Elijah!" Immediately one of them ran and got a sponge, filled it with sour wine, fixed it on a reed, and offered Him a drink. But the rest said, "Let's see if Elijah comes to save Him!" Jesus shouted again with a loud voice and gave up His spirit. Suddenly, the curtain of the sanctuary was split in two from top to bottom;

THE ORIGIN AND PURPOSE OF PRAYER

the earth quaked and the rocks were split. The tombs also were opened and many bodies of the saints who had gone to their rest were raised. And they came out of the tombs after His resurrection, entered the holy city, and appeared to many.
(Matt 27:45-53 HCSB)

The holy cry of the Lord Jesus changed everything for the human race. It tore from the top to the bottom, the curtains of the sanctuary that hinders humans from entering into the Holy of Holies, where the Shekinah glory of the Godhead dwells.

When the Lord cried out with a loud voice and gave up his spirit, he met the lawful righteous requirement of God's law for the redemption of the human souls from sin and death.

Romans 4:25, says he was delivered up for our trespasses and he was raised to life for our justification. Through his sacrificial work on the cross, he disarmed the devil and took from him, the dominion mandate he stole from mankind in the beginning. To achieve all these, the above portion of scriptures says he cried out with a loud voice to the Father who alone was able to save him from death, and he was heard because of his reverence.

In those days Hezeki'ah became sick and was at the point of death. And Isaiah the prophet the son of Amoz came to him, and said to him, "Thus says the Lord: Set your house in order; for you shall die, you shall not recover." Then Hezeki'ah turned his face to the wall, and prayed to the Lord, and said, "Remember now, O Lord, I beseech thee, how I have walked before thee in faithfulness and with a whole heart, and have done what is good in thy sight." And Hezeki'ah wept bitterly. Then the word of the Lord came to Isaiah: "Go and say to Hezeki'ah,

HOLY CRY

Thus says the Lord, the God of David your father: I have heard your prayer, I have seen your tears; behold, I will add fifteen years to your life. I will deliver you and this city out of the hand of the king of Assyria, and defend this city. "This is the sign to you from the Lord, that the Lord will do this thing that he has promised: Behold, I will make the shadow cast by the declining sun on the dial of Ahaz turn back ten steps." So the sun turned back on the dial the ten steps by which it had declined. (Is.38:1-8RSV)

When the great prophet Isaiah prophesied by the word of the Lord that king Hezekiah would not recover from his sickness, the Bible declares that the king turned his face to the wall and cried out to the Lord in prayer. He wept bitterly before God, and the holy cry he raised caused the Lord to cancel the death verdict that he had pronounced against him through the mouth of his servant, the prophet Isaiah. In addition, God healed him, and added fifteen more years to his life. The holy cry that the king raised turned things around for him. Something miraculous and astonishing always happen when people engage in the holy cry.

In my other book, *Understanding the Art of Prayer (Revisited)*, under the heading, "Dynamics of Prayer," I explained how Hannah the wife of Elkanah, whose womb the Lord closed so she could not have children, used the miracle-working power of prayer to unblock her womb and turn her situation around.

The passage relates how she went with her husband Elkanah and her rival Peninnah to Shiloh every year to worship and make sacrifices to the Lord. On the day Elkanah presented his sacrifice, he would give portions of the meat to Peninnah his wife and each of her children.

THE ORIGIN AND PURPOSE OF PRAYER

But to Hannah, he would give double portion because he loved her, even though the Lord had closed her womb. So her rival Peninnah took advantage of the fact she could not bear children and provoked Hannah until she wept and would not eat. This happened each time they went to the house of God at Shiloh.

There was a certain man from Ramathaim, a Zuphite from the hill country of Ephraim, whose name was Elkanah son of Jeroham, the son of Elihu, the son of Tohu, the son of Zuph, an Ephraimite. He had two wives; one was called Hannah and the other Peninnah. Peninnah had children, but Hannah had none. Year after year this man went up from his town to worship and sacrifice to the Lord Almighty at Shiloh, where Hophni and Phinehas, the two sons of Eli, were priests of the Lord. Whenever the day came for Elkanah to sacrifice, he would give portions of the meat to his wife Peninnah and to all her sons and daughters. But to Hannah he gave a double portion because he loved her, and the Lord had closed her womb. And because the Lord had closed her womb, her rival kept provoking her in order to irritate her. This went on year after year. Whenever Hannah went up to the house of the Lord, her rival provoked her till she wept and would not eat. Elkanah her husband would say to her, "Hannah, why are you weeping? Why don't you eat? Why are you downhearted? Don't I mean more to you than ten sons?"
(1 Sam.1:1-8NIV)

One day, after they had finished eating and drinking, Hannah was deeply distressed and she wept bitterly before the Lord in prayer moving only her lips, but her voice was not heard. Eli, the high priest who was sitting beside the entrance of the Tabernacle, observed her moving only her lips as she prayed in her heart, and he thought she was drunk.

HOLY CRY

He said to her, "How long are you going to stay drunk? Put your wine away from you."

Hannah answered, "No, my lord, I am a woman who is deeply troubled. I have drunk neither wine nor strong drink, but have poured out my soul before the Lord. Don't think I am a wicked woman, for I have been praying out of great anguish and sorrow." Then Eli answered, "Go in peace, and may the God of Israel grant the request you have asked of him."

Once when they had finished eating and drinking in Shiloh, Hannah stood up. Now Eli the priest was sitting on a chair by the doorpost of the Lord's temple. In bitterness of soul Hannah wept much and prayed to the Lord. And she made a vow, saying, "O Lord Almighty, if you will only look upon your servant's misery and remember me, and not forget your servant but give her a son, then I will give him to the Lord for all the days of his life, and no razor will ever be used on his head." As she kept on praying to the Lord, Eli observed her mouth. Hannah was praying in her heart, and her lips were moving but her voice was not heard. Eli thought she was drunk and said to her, "How long will you keep on getting drunk? Get rid of your wine." "Not so, my lord," Hannah replied, "I am a woman who is deeply troubled. I have not been drinking wine or beer; I was pouring out my soul to the Lord. Do not take your servant for a wicked woman; I have been praying here out of my great anguish and grief." Eli answered, "Go in peace, and may the God of Israel grant you what you have asked of him." She said, "May your servant find favor in your eyes." Then she went her way and ate something, and her face was no longer downcast. Early the next morning they arose and worshiped before the Lord and then went back to their home at Ramah.

THE ORIGIN AND PURPOSE OF PRAYER

Elkanah lay with Hannah his wife, and the Lord remembered her. So in the course of time Hannah conceived and gave birth to a son. She named him Samuel, saying, "Because I asked the Lord for him."
(1 Sam.1:9-20NIV)

Then she went, ate something, and her face was no longer sad. The whole family got up early the next morning and went to worship the Lord before returning to their home at Ramah. God remembered her and in due time, she conceived and gave birth to a son who she named Samuel, saying, "I asked the Lord for him."

The holy cry of Hannah to God because of the distress, bitterness, anguish and sorrow that her rival Peninnah caused her for not having children, made the Lord to remember her and opened her womb so she could have children. In the end, Hannah's life was completely turned around for good because she raised her voice to God in a holy cry, and the Lord granted her desires.

The book of Jonah describes how God sent his servant to the great city Nineveh to announce the imminent judgement that would come on the people because of their wicked practices. Instead of the prophet Jonah to obey God's word, he bought a ticket for a ship going to Tarshish and went on board in order to flee from the presence of the Lord.

For this reason, God sent a great wind to the sea that threatened to break the ship apart. Everyone in the ship was so afraid that each person cried out to his respective god, but Jonah went down below deck, lay and fell deeply asleep. When the captain saw him, he said, "How can you sleep at a time like this? Get up and pray to your god! Maybe he will pay attention to us and spare our lives."

HOLY CRY

Finally they decided to cast lots to find out who is responsible for the calamity, and the lots fell on Jonah. When they asked him what they should do to calm the sea, he asked them to throw him into the sea. Verse 14 says that the people cried out to God to forgive their action as they threw Jonah into the raging sea, but the man of God did not pray until he had spent three days and night in the belly of the fish God sent to swallow him up. While in the belly of the fish, Jonah came to himself and turned the place into a platform for prayer.

While in the belly of the fish, the prophet Jonah cried out to God. As soon as he finished praying, the Lord commanded the fish to vomit him to dry land. This reveals that the solution to Jonah's trouble, hardship, and affliction was prayer. However, that was the one thing he refused to do until he found himself in the belly of the fish for three days and nights.

Jonah 2:1-10 relates the nature of his prayer and the results it produced. Prayer works wonders! It changes lives and situations! Don't wait until things fall apart before you cry out to God. Just as prayer brings healing, deliverance and restoration, it also has the ability to prevent negative things from happening in your life. If you can cry out to the Lord today, your holy cry would give you what no other means can do for you.

Then Jonah prayed to the Lord his God from inside the fish. He said, "I cried out to the Lord in my great trouble, and he answered me. I called to you from the land of the dead, and Lord, you heard me! You threw me into the ocean depths, and I sank down to the heart of the sea. The mighty waters engulfed me; I was buried beneath your wild and stormy waves.

THE ORIGIN AND PURPOSE OF PRAYER

Then I said, 'O Lord, you have driven me from your presence. Yet I will look once more toward your holy Temple.' "I sank beneath the waves, and the waters closed over me. Seaweed wrapped itself around my head. I sank down to the very roots of the mountains. I was imprisoned in the earth, whose gates lock shut forever. But you, O Lord my God, snatched me from the jaws of death! As my life was slipping away, I remembered the Lord. And my earnest prayer went out to you in your holy Temple. Those who worship false gods turn their backs on all God's mercies. But I will offer sacrifices to you with songs of praise, and I will fulfill all my vows. For my salvation comes from the Lord alone." Then the Lord ordered the fish to spit Jonah out onto the beach.
(Jonah 2:1-6NLT)

The last example I would like to use to illustrate this point is that of Jacob. Since I used the same story to explain a similar idea in my previous book, I would repeat almost what I said in the other book.

Genesis 32:2-26, informs us of how Jacob sent messengers to his brother Esau, who was living in the region of Seir in the land of Edom, so that he might obtain favor and forgiveness from him; for Jacob had stolen Esau's blessing before he fled to Paddan Aram to the house of his mother's father Bethuel. This happened when his mother Rebekah heard that Esau was planning to kill Jacob, so she asked him to flee to her brother Laban in Haran and remain there with him until his brother's anger subsided and he forgot what Jacob did to him (Gen.27:42-45).

Jacob stayed with Laban until God commanded him to go back to the land of his fathers (Gen.31:3). After twenty years with Laban, Jacob decided to go back home.

HOLY CRY

On the way, he sent messengers and gifts ahead of him to Esau to appease his fury because he was afraid of him. Jacob gave the following instruction to the messengers he sent, "Your servant Jacob says, 'I have been staying with Laban and have remained there till now. I have cattle and donkeys, sheep and goats, menservants and maidservants. Now I am sending this message to my lord that I may find favor in your eyes.'"

When the messengers returned to Jacob, and told him that his brother Esau was coming with four hundred men to meet him, he was greatly afraid and distressed. He thought Esau would avenge the wrong he did to him by stealing his birthright and blessings. For this reason, Jacob divided his household, along with the flocks, herds, and camels into two groups, thinking that if his brother Esau attacked one group, the other group might escape. Having done that, he cried out to the Lord in prayer:

God of my father Abraham and God of my father Isaac, the Lord, who said to me, "Go back to your land and to your family, and I will cause you to prosper," I am unworthy of all the kindness and faithfulness You have shown Your servant. Indeed, I crossed over this Jordan with my staff, and now I have become two camps. Please rescue me from the hand of my brother Esau, for I am afraid of him; otherwise, he may come and attack me, the mothers, and their children. You have said, "I will cause you to prosper, and I will make your offspring like the sand of the sea, which cannot be counted."
(Gen. 32:9-12 HCSB)

After the holy cry, Jacob selected a gift from his possession to present to his brother Esau, so that he might use it to appease him for stealing his birthright and blessing.

THE ORIGIN AND PURPOSE OF PRAYER

He also sent all he had ahead and he remained alone in the camp. Suddenly, a man visited him and wrestled with him till daybreak. When he realized that he could not prevail against Jacob, he touched his hip and put it out of joint.

Remember, Jacob had an issue with his brother for stealing his blessing and when he heard Esau was coming to him with four hundred men, fear gripped him, so he prayed for God to deliver him from his brother's hand. God had also instructed him to return to his father's house and possess the land he promised to his father Abraham. But Jacob had taken it through deception, by pretending to be Esau when Isaac prayed for him. The Lord needed to fix all of that before Jacob reached home.

So he visited Jacob while he was alone, because Jacob could not face his brother Esau and possess the land the way he was. Some things needed to be corrected before he could possess the blessing. I believe God didn't go to Jacob to engage in a fight but to help him because Jacob had cried out to him for help against his brother, who he thought would kill him for the wrong he did in the past.

Jacob's cry to the Lord for help because of the difficult and desperate situation he was in at the time, caused God to appear in the form of human, and visited him to fix some issues in his life. This is one of the reasons I say that the "holy cry" is a cry that changes lives and situations. It provokes the miraculous, signs and wonders.

Are you going through some challenges in life? Does it look like your world is coming to an end?

HOLY CRY

Does it look like the enemies have taken control of something that belongs to you? Has your place of honor, glory, blessing, promotion, joy, peace and fulfillment, becomes that of shame, humiliation, pains, demotion, frustration, sadness, regret, lost, disappointment etc. don't merely cry and weep about it, for that won't help the situation at all. I encourage you to raise a holy cry to God today, and watch him do the impossible for you.

Many people have used the weapon of prayer to change their lives and situations. It has happened before, and it will continue to happen. You are not alone in this matter, turn to God, and cry out to him in prayer. The Lord has the ability to turn things around for you, but you retain the right to act in this planet. Connect your right to act with God's ability to do things, through a holy cry and turn things around in your life. Give it a try, it works like magic! And your life will never again remain the same!

Is anyone among you suffering? Let him pray. Is anyone cheerful? Let him sing praise. Is anyone among you sick? Let him call for the elders of the church, and let them pray over him, anointing him with oil in the name of the Lord. And the prayer of faith will save the one who is sick, and the Lord will raise him up. And if he has committed sins, he will be forgiven.

(Jas. 5:13-16 ESV)

IMPORTANT ABBREVIATIONS

Gen.	Genesis
Ex.	Exodus
Lev.	Leviticus
Num.	Numbers
Deut.	Deuteronomy
Josh.	Joshua
Judg.	Judges
1Sa.	1Samuel
2Sa.	2Samuel
1Ki.	1Kings
2Ki.	2Kings
1Ch.	1Chronicles
2Ch.	2Chronicles
Neh.	Nehemiah
Esth.	Esther
Ps.	Psalms
Pr.	Proverbs
Ecc.	Ecclesiastics
SoS	Song of Songs
Is.	Isaiah
Jer.	Jeremiah
Lam.	Lamentations
Ezek.	Ezekiel
Dan.	Daniel
Hos.	Hosea
Jon.	Jonah
Mic.	Micah
Nah.	Nahum
Hab.	Habakkuk
Zeph.	Zephaniah
Hag.	Haggai
Zec.	Zechariah

Matt.	Matthew
Mk.	Mark
Lk.	Luke
Jn.	John
Rom.	Romans
1Co.	1Corinthians
2Co.	2Corinthians
Gal.	Galatians
Eph.	Ephesians
Phi.	Philippians
Col.	Colossians
1Thes.	1Thessalonians
2Thes.	2Thessalonians
1Tim.	1Timothy
2Tim.	2Timothy
Heb.	Hebrews
Jas.	James
1Pet.	1Peter
2Pet.	2Peter
1Jn.	1John
2Jn.	2John
3Jn.	3John
Rev.	Revelation

PRAYER OF SALVATION

The gospel message also known as the word of faith, belief and open confession play distinct roles in the salvation process, according to Romans 10:8-10. The word of faith produces the faith we need to please God and be at peace with him (Heb.11:6), believing that God raised Jesus from death causes him to impute his righteousness that is by faith to us (Rom.4:22-25). Confessing the lordship of Jesus makes God to infuse our spirit with his eternal life for rebirth.

Salvation does not come by merely verbalizing the *Sinner's Prayer* without faith in Christ atoning sacrifice that comes from hearing the gospel message, repentance from dead works, and open confession of Jesus Christ as Lord and Savior.

1. Believe in your heart that Christ is the Son of the living God.
2. Believe he died on the cross for your sins and iniquities.
3. Believe that God raised him from the dead after three days for your justification.
4. Believe he is at the right hand of the Father in heaven interceding for you.
5. Believe that only Christ has the legitimate right to give eternal life to humans.
6. Ask him to forgive your sins and wash you by his blood.
7. Openly declare him lord of your life from the depth of your heart.
8. Invite him to come and dwell in you.
9. Ask him to write your name in the book of life.

And this is the testimony: God has given us eternal life, and this life is in his Son. He who has the Son has life; he who does not have the Son of God does not have life.

I write these things to you who believe in the name of the Son of God so that you may know that you have eternal life.
(1 Jn. 5:11-14 NIV)

If you confess with your mouth the Lord Jesus and believe in your heart that God has raised Him from the dead, you will be saved. For with the heart one believes unto righteousness, and with the mouth confession is made unto salvation.
(Rom.10:9-10 NKJV)

Salvation is found in no one else, for there is no other name under heaven given to men by which we must be saved.
(Acts 4:12 NIV)

If we confess our sins, He is faithful and righteous to forgive us our sins and to cleanse us from all unrighteousness.
(1Jn.1:9-10 HCSB)

Once you finish reading the above portion of scriptures, you can make the following confession with me from the depth of your heart. Believe it as you speak, and you shall be saved in Jesus name.

Dear Jesus,

I believe that you died on the cross for my sins, and rose on the third day for my justification. You took away my sins, iniquities, infirmities and blotted out the handwriting of ordinances that were against me by your blood. You were bruised for my transgressions, and became a curse for me in order to redeem my soul from death.

I beseech you Lord to come into my life today, and make my heart your dwelling place. I confess you now as my Lord and Savior. Write my name in the book of life, and make me a new person. Thank you Lord Jesus for saving me. Amen

Congratulation!

Therefore confess your sins to each other and pray for each other so that you may be healed. The prayer of a righteous man is powerful and effective. Elijah was a man just like us. He prayed earnestly that it would not rain, and it did not rain on the land for three and a half years. Again he prayed, and the heavens gave rain, and the earth produced its crops.

(Jas. 5:16-18NIV)

Follow me on **f** Caesar Benedo
Email.caesben11@yahoo.com

Dépot Légal N° 8008 du 14 / 07 / 2015
Bibliothèque National, 3ème Trimestre

www.ingramcontent.com/pod-product-compliance
Lightning Source LLC
Chambersburg PA
CBHW061440040426
42450CB00007B/1139